Generalist Case Management

A Workbook for Skill Development

Generalist Case Management

A Workbook for Skill Development

Tricia McClam
University of Tennessee

Marianne Woodside
University of Tennessee

The authors contributed equally to the writing of this book.

THOMSON

WADSWORTH

Australia • Brazil • Canada • Mexico • Singapore • Spain
United Kingdom • United States

THOMSON

WADSWORTH

Generalist Case Management: A Workbook for Skill Development
Tricia McClam and Marianne Woodside

Senior Acquisitions Editor: *Marquita Flemming*
Assistant Editor: *Samantha Shook*
Technology Project Manager: *Inna Fedoseyeva*
Marketing Manager: *Megan McCullough*
Senior Marketing Communications Manager: *Shemikra Britt*
Project Manager, Editorial Production: *Christy Krueger*
Creative Director: *Rob Hugel*
Art Director: *Vernon Boes*
Print Buyer: *Karen Hunt*

Permissions Editor: *Audrey Pettengil*
Production Service: *Buuji Inc.*
Production Editor: *Sara Dovre Wudali*
Copy Editor: *Pat Tompkins*
Cover Designer: *Paula Goldstein*
Cover Image: © *Gary Kempston c/o theispot.com*
Cover Printer: *Thomson West*
Compositor: *Interactive Composition Corporation*
Printer: *Thomson West*

Printed in the United States of America
1 2 3 4 5 6 7 10 09 08 07 06

ISBN 0-534-52141-X

Thomson Higher Education
10 Davis Drive
Belmont, CA 94002-3098
USA

For more information about our products, contact us at:
Thomson Learning Academic Resource Center
1-800-423-0563
For permission to use material from this text or product, submit a request online at http://www.thomsonrights.com.
Any additional questions about permissions can be submitted by e-mail to thomsonrights@thomson.com.

Contents....................

Chapter 10   Ethical and Legal Issues   170

Chapter 11   Surviving as a Case Manager   182

Preface

Our purpose in writing this workbook was to provide opportunities for our students to think about, practice, apply, and reflect on some of the many skills that are integral to successful case management. A second purpose was to reinforce many of the case management concepts introduced in *Generalist Case Management,* a text that provides an overview of case management; the requisite knowledge, roles, models, and skills; the organizational perspective; and the ethical and legal issues in case management. Our students like case studies, self-assessments, and web-based learning. We hope you will, too.

As you use this text, keep in mind that it is a workbook. This means that you will find plenty of space to record answers, complete exercises, and develop plans. It has been designed for you, the student. Make it yours by underlining, highlighting, and writing in the margins.

Features

All chapters in this workbook have a number of common features that will help you extend your learning beyond *Generalist Case Management.* All chapters begin with some type of pretest (answers provided) to reinforce the main ideas of *Generalist Case Management.* A chapter summary follows the pretest. Exercises relevant to each chapter provide practice opportunities that relate to various case management skills. Among them are writing plans and case notes, examining tests, applying time management strategies, and using case management models. Web-based activities also appear in each chapter to provide additional readings, vignettes, role-playing opportunities, and cases. Next is a section that explores a concept, idea, client group, or issue in more depth. Additional exercises focus on a combination of textbook concepts, case studies, and new information from this section.

All chapters conclude with a focus on self-assessment. These questions will help you ascertain what you know, what questions remain, and how you believe you will use the information in the chapter. The questions will also enhance your development of professional values, skills, and knowledge. We believe that these questions represent the tone of the entire workbook—that of exploration and learning. They will also encourage both reflection and continued education by prospective case managers.

In More Depth

An example of the necessity of continued education is a section in each chapter unique to this workbook—"In More Depth." For example, Chapter 1 offers a focus on the strengths-based approach to case management. The section in Chapter 2 expands students' thinking about the influences of legislation on day-to-day case management responsibilities. Topics explored in more detail in other chapters include children as a client group; PACT as a case management model; advocacy; ethical issues that may arise when working with individuals with HIV/AIDS; and vicarious trauma.

We hope that as you read about these topics, you will begin to think about other topics that are unique to the needs of different client groups, the human service problems that case managers encounter, and the changing times and political climate in which we live. Time and space limited our choices to these 11 topics, but we know that immigration, poverty, natural disasters, the living wage, aging baby boomers, Medicare and Social Security are among the future issues that will impact case management. So once again, we encourage you to commit to continued education.

Acknowledgments

Many people contribute to a project as diverse as this workbook. Our colleagues and students at the University of Tennessee have encouraged our efforts. Dr. Steve McCallum, our department head, has also been supportive of our work. Ellen Carruth and Angie Fuss, graduate students, assisted us with various research efforts.

We could not have completed the manuscript without the help of many human service professionals. Many thanks to the case managers in urban multicultural areas across the country who guided our thinking and provided specific examples and cases for this text as they shared their expertise and professional knowledge.

We have a talented group of friends at Brooks/Cole that we work with, and we acknowledge their guidance, encouragement, and contributions to the development of this project. They include Marquita Flemming, Senior Acquisitions Editor; Samantha Shook, Assistant Editor; Meghan McCullough, Marketing Manager; Inna Fedoseyeva, Technology Project Manager; Christy Krueger, Content Project Manager; Audrey Pettengill, Permissions Editor; and Karen Hunt, Print Buyer.

Introduction to Case Management

Chapter 1 in *Generalist Case Management* presents an overview of the case management process, the components that appear throughout the process, and the principles and goals that guide the process. The following chapter provides opportunities for you to work with these ideas as you apply them to "real" service delivery.

 **Pretest**

When you finish reading Chapter 1 in *Generalist Case Management*, answer the following questions and complete the items.

1. List the three phases of case management:

   _____

   _____

   _____

   _____

2. Some case managers object to the terms "case management" and "case manager." Why?

   _____

   _____

   _____

3. Identify an example of documentation in Roy's case and explain its purpose:

   _____

   _____

   _____

4. How and why does data gathering occur in assessment and planning?

   _____

   _____

   _____

5. How does a recipient of services participate in each of the three phases of case management?

   _____

   _____

   _____

Chapter Summary

Traditionally, helping professionals view linking clients to services as a process. Changes in the conceptualization of case management and the roles of case managers have been evident in the language used to describe service delivery. For example, some case managers reject their title because it implies they "manage" clients. Many prefer the job title "care coordinator."

Today, case management occurs in three phases: assessment, planning, and implementation. Each phase of case management requires specific knowledge and skills that the case manager should possess to meet the needs of his or her client. Throughout the process of case management, flexibility and client involvement are critical, as the case manager works toward the goal of client empowerment.

Case management includes three important elements: case review, report writing and documentation, and client participation. Each helps the case manager uphold the principles and goals of case management. Integration of services, continuity of care, equal access to services, quality care, client empowerment, and evaluation are principles and goals that have come from the early work of helping professionals and later federal legislation to describe current practices in case management. The process of case management is collaborative, involving the client as a partner throughout the different phases. The process is also

Cyclic

nonlinear; the case manager must be able to reassess the strengths and needs of the client depending on the changing contexts of the client's life. The case manager must continuously strive toward upholding the principles of case management to provide the most helpful and supportive services.

The following exercises offer opportunities for you to think about the phases of case management.

Exercise 1: The Phases of Case Management

1. Review the section in Chapter 1 about the three phases of case management: assessment, planning, and implementation.
2. A description of ABEL Case Management, Inc., an organization that provides both community and home-based care for elderly clients in Wahiawi, Hawaii, is on the website which accompanies this book: www.thomsonedu.com/counseling/mcclam, Chapter 1, Link 1.
3. As you read this description of case management, think about its three phases.
4. Based upon the information provided about ABEL Case Management, what conclusions can you draw about how this organization uses the three phases of case management?

Assessment:

_____

_____

_____

_____

Planning:

_____

_____

_____

_____

Implementation:

_____

_____

_____

_____

Exercise 2: Three Components of Case Management

1. Read the three components of case management: case review, documentation, and client participation.
2. Review Roy R. Johnson's case in Chapter 1 of *Generalist Case Management*.
3. Think about each of the three components of case management.
   Case review:
4. How does case review occur in Roy R. Johnson's case?

_____

_____

_____

_____

5. When does it occur?

_____

_____

_____

_____

Documentation:

6. Identify the documentation and report writing that is part of Roy's case record.

_____

_____

_____

_____

7. What reports and documents are in the case file?

_____

_____

_____

_____

Client participation:

8. List the ways that Roy participates in case management:

_____

_____

_____

_____

9. In what other ways could he participate?

_____

_____

_____

_____

•••••••••• ● Exercise 3: Agency Practice

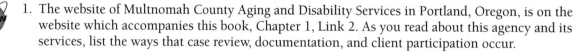

1. The website of Multnomah County Aging and Disability Services in Portland, Oregon, is on the website which accompanies this book, Chapter 1, Link 2. As you read about this agency and its services, list the ways that case review, documentation, and client participation occur.

Case review:

_____

_____

_____

_____

Documentation:

_____

_____

_____

_____

Client participation:

_____

_____

_____

_____

 ## Exercise 4: Client Participation

Client participation is a particularly critical component of case management today, in part, because of concerns about accountability and customer satisfaction. Many agencies find creative ways to engage clients while others limit client participation.

1. Read the description of AIDS Partnership Michigan on the website which accompanies this book, Chapter 1, Link 3, with the concept of client participation in mind. According to this agency's program literature, AIDS Partnership Michigan is the state's central resource for information and referral about HIV/AIDS and the largest service provider in Michigan. One of its goals is "to simplify client access to services and to develop new programs to meet the community's changing needs." Case management, one of its primary services, is also described on the website which accompanies this book, Chapter 1, Link 3.
2. Imagine you are a case manager at AIDS Partnership Michigan. Describe how you would engage your clients in participating in service delivery.

_____

_____

_____

3. For each instance of client participation you identify, explain the benefits to the client and the case management process.

_____

_____

_____

_____

 ## Exercise 5: Principles and Goals

1. Review the six principles and goals of case management described in Chapter 1 of the *Generalist Case Management* text.

2. Select one of the agencies presented on the website which accompanies this book, Links 1, 2, and 3. Review its website.

3. For the six principles and goals listed next, explain how each applies to the agency you selected.

Integration of services:

_____

_____

_____

Continuity of care:

_____

_____

_____

Equal access to services:

_____

_____

_____

Quality care:

_____

_____

_____

Client empowerment:

_____

_____

_____

Evaluation:

_____

_____

_____

⬤ Exercise 6: Case Management Today

 Go to the website which accompanies this book, Chapter 1, Links 4 and 5, and listen and watch as Marianne interviews Bobby, who has been both a case manager and a supervisor. Then answer the following questions:

1. How does Bobby's description of case management match what you have read?

_____

_____

_____

2. What is different?

_____

_____

_____

3. If you could interview Bobby, what would you ask him?

_____

_____

_____

•••••••••••• ● In More Depth: Eye of the Tiger (Positively Speaking!)

Traditional case management attempted to coordinate the care of people who were deinstitutionalized in the 1960s. It has continued as a significant concept in mental health practice since that time. Today, the context in which case management operates is shifting. One indication of this change is the rejection by many case managers of the idea that clients are "cases" to be "managed." Another is a redirection of assessment of the client from problem focused to strengths based. Here we will explore this second shift, including its influence on the stages of planning and implementation.

What is the strengths-based approach to case management? It is exactly what its name implies—an emphasis on strengths, resources, coping, possibilities, and resilience rather than problems, pathologies, and liabilities. This perspective to helping and to case management, in particular, rests on the following assumptions identified by Saleeby (1997):

✦ All people and environments possess strengths that can be marshaled to improve lives.
✦ Client motivation is fostered by a consistent emphasis on strengths as defined by the client.
✦ Discovering strengths involves cooperation between client and worker.
✦ This approach focuses the helper on discovering how the client has survived in the past.
✦ All environments contain resources.

How does strengths-based case management work? The foundation of the strengths-based perspective is choice—choice about goals, interventions (methods or strategies), and context (outpatient, individual, group). In the case management process, this translates to the client as case manager. Necessary conditions for this to occur are a belief in the right of the individual for self-determination, responsibility for his or her actions, and respect for his or her preferences and choices. It also requires the client to take an active role regarding assessment, planning, and implementation. The helper also has obligations, and these include the suspension of judgment about the client and his or her circumstances.

Let's examine the strengths-based perspective in relation to the case management process.

Assessment

A strengths-based approach to the assessment phase focuses on the positive characteristics, abilities, and experiences of the client to build upon them in addressing current problems. The case manager identifies these by asking clients to recall how they have solved problems in the past and to describe successes at home, school, work, and in relationships. This discussion is part of the problem identification phase but shifts the emphasis from problems or deficit thinking to a more positive, client-focused position.

This approach to assessment takes time and calls for patience and facilitation from the case manager. There is a dual focus at this point. One is to collect information about the client's needs and resources; the second is to assess client functioning and the client's social network, for example. In the strengths-based approach, the case manager is most interested in the client's resources and abilities. To identify these, the client may need prompting to recall past successful behaviors and situations. The following examples of statements or questions encourage this recall: "Tell me about a time when you faced a similar problem." "What do you consider your most important ability?" "What have you learned from your friends and family?" "What do you enjoy doing?"

Taking time to explore the client's responses has other benefits. Identifying strengths fosters motivation. For example, focusing on positives rather than negatives empowers the client to believe that change is possible and that he or she has the abilities and resources to make this happen. This positive approach also helps build rapport and the relationship between the client and the case manager. The client leaves this session with hope that needs will be met and with confidence in the case manager and the relationship.

During this phase, the case manager also assesses the client's readiness for change in the areas the client has identified. Older models depended on the case manager to inform the client what to do. The noncompliant client was then labeled as resistant. Strengths-based approaches consider change as a process that begins with two stages. The first is precontemplation at which point there has been no thought about change, and the second is contemplation, where considering change begins although probably with some ambivalence.

There are a number of tools to assist with strengths identification. They include questionnaires, surveys, and forms that may be completed by the client, the family, the case manager, or a combination of those involved. Figure 1 is an example of a simple form. The Strengths Questionnaire (see Figure 2) is a self-assessment instrument that is intended to alert the client and the case manager to areas of perceived strength (McQuaide & Ehrenreich, 1997, p. 209). It is not a psychometrically validated scale so the meaning of responses must be corroborated through interviews, history, and other clinical work. Other approaches are more complex and encompass the following seven domains: living arrangements, leisure/recreational, vocational/educational, health/medical, social support, emotional/behavioral, and financial. You will see how these work when you read about Homeless Joe. Whatever the approach, the goal of the strengths-based approach is the identification of client strengths and resources.

Planning

The second phase of the case management process is planning. An understanding of strengths is essential to effectively plan. The strengths, abilities, and resources of the client become part of plan development. In addition, all environments contain resources, and these are identified and incorporated into the planning process. These may exist in the home, the extended family, the place of employment, the place of worship, the community, or a mix of several of these. Increasing the number of available resources identified has a direct bearing on the success of the plan: the more resources to support the client's efforts, the greater the possibilities for change.

During this phase the client–case manager collaboration continues and becomes a stronger and more positive force in the case management process. A critical part of this collaboration is client participation in determining both short-term and long-term goals that are compatible with the client's values and strengths. These goals are also realistic given the client's abilities and available resources. And they are stated positively, again a basic tenet of the strengths-based approach. Finally, the client provides input about updates based on changes in any conditions that affect the client, the plan, and the case management process. Assuming this responsibility engenders client participation and is one way that the transfer of case management responsibilities to the client occurs.

Implementation

Several approaches to implementation are grounded in client strengths. Among them are harm reduction, solution-focused intervention, cognitive-behavioral strategies, and motivational interviewing. The hallmark of any strengths-based intervention is choice. Specifically, the client has options in terms of the goals determined during the planning phase, the interventions or methods employed to bring about change, and the context of intervention (e.g., outpatient, inpatient, group, individual, etc.). The possibilities available to the client emphasize the values of self-determination and responsibility. The case manager maximizes any benefits of these choices by respecting the client's preferences and choices, further solidifying the relationship and affirming the client's active role in the case management process.

Another critical component of intervention is incorporating the resources that have been identified. These may be community-based resources, such as services provided by other agencies for which the client is eligible, or the resource may be one or more family members who will support the client's efforts. In fact, the resource may have been available but not directed to or activated for the client's benefit. Making use of every available support enhances the client's chances for success.

Let's examine a specific intervention to see how it works. Motivational interviewing is a strategy that enhances the client's desire to change by exploring and resolving ambivalence. Although first used with problem drinkers, its use has expanded to a number of different problems, including smoking, bulimia, and

FIGURE 1

Problem _____

Consumer Strengths	Consumer Resources	Barriers

....

FIGURE 2 ◆ STRENGTHS QUESTIONNAIRE

This questionnaire contains possible true statements about you that we may not have discussed yet in session. Read each statement carefully. For each statement, fill in the square next to the response that best represents your opinion.

SD = *strongly disagree* or the statement is definitely false. D = *disagree* or the statement is mostly false.
N = *neutral* on the statement, that is, you cannot decide A = *agree* or the statement is mostly true.
or the statement is about equally true and false. SA = *strongly agree* or the statement is definitely true.

	SD	D	N	A	SA
1. I am a creative person.	☐	☐	☐	☐	☐
2. I am curious person.	☐	☐	☐	☐	☐
3. I am able to love other people.	☐	☐	☐	☐	☐
4. I can anticipate a problem and come up with a plan to solve it.	☐	☐	☐	☐	☐
5. I don't let other people's opinions of my actions control me.	☐	☐	☐	☐	☐
6. I have good common sense in most situations.	☐	☐	☐	☐	☐
7. My goals for myself are realistic.	☐	☐	☐	☐	☐
8. I have an accurate view of my strengths and weaknesses.	☐	☐	☐	☐	☐
9. Other people's behavior is usually predictable to me.	☐	☐	☐	☐	☐
10. I can usually predict when situations are safe or dangerous.	☐	☐	☐	☐	☐
11. I am self-aware and like to learn about myself.	☐	☐	☐	☐	☐
12. I think about my mistakes and learn from them.	☐	☐	☐	☐	☐
13. If something is bothering me I can channel my energies into something constructive.	☐	☐	☐	☐	☐
14. My sense of humor helps me deal with stressful situations.	☐	☐	☐	☐	☐
15. If I can't control a certain situation I can "turn it over" and stop worrying about it.	☐	☐	☐	☐	☐
16. I can choose my battles.	☐	☐	☐	☐	☐
17. I have techniques I use to calm myself when I am upset.	☐	☐	☐	☐	☐
18. My self-esteem is usually high.	☐	☐	☐	☐	☐

	SD	D	N	A	SA
19. I can usually control my impulses.	☐	☐	☐	☐	☐
20. I am usually a flexible person.	☐	☐	☐	☐	☐
21. I am a more active than passive person.	☐	☐	☐	☐	☐
22. I usually trust other people.	☐	☐	☐	☐	☐
23. I believe the world is more good than bad.	☐	☐	☐	☐	☐
24. I usually feel I can cope well in new situations.	☐	☐	☐	☐	☐
25. I believe I am not a victim.	☐	☐	☐	☐	☐
26. I can deal with the unknown.	☐	☐	☐	☐	☐
27. My life has meaning and purpose.	☐	☐	☐	☐	☐
28. I am easy going.	☐	☐	☐	☐	☐
29. I am patient.	☐	☐	☐	☐	☐
30. Even when things are hard, I persevere.	☐	☐	☐	☐	☐
31. I can usually tolerate not knowing how things will turn out.	☐	☐	☐	☐	☐
32. I am a "positive thinker."	☐	☐	☐	☐	☐
33. I take responsibility for my own decisions.	☐	☐	☐	☐	☐
34. Other people usually like me.	☐	☐	☐	☐	☐
35. I can enjoy being alone.	☐	☐	☐	☐	☐
36. I have a confidante.	☐	☐	☐	☐	☐
37. I have created a supportive network of friends.	☐	☐	☐	☐	☐
38. I can go to others for help, as appropriate.	☐	☐	☐	☐	☐

39. What do you believe your strengths are in the state of relationships and in work? _____

_____

_____

40. What would people who know you list as your strengths?

_____

_____

Source: "The Strengths Questionnaire" McQuaide, S., & Ehrenreich, J. H. (1997). Assessing client strengths. *Families in Society,* 78(2), 209. Reprinted with permission.

domestic violence, and to a variety of settings such as medical practice, child welfare, and community-based organizations. Its goal is to help clients change by providing a way for them to see themselves and the costs of their behavior and to find the motivation to change the targeted behaviors. Motivational interviewing facilitates client change not by admitting the problem or finding solutions but rather by focusing on identifying what is preventing the client from changing.

The goal of motivational interviewing strategies is to increase motivation, not to get answers. The interview begins by determining the client's current level of motivation or readiness to change. One way to determine this is to ask, "If on a scale of 1 to 10, 1 is not at all motivated to give up smoking and 10 is 100% motivated to give it up, what number would you give yourself at the moment?" (Van Wormer & Davis, 2003, p. 80). Following up with an inquiry about "why a 4 rather than a 1" will lead to the identification of positive reasons for change. "What would it take for your confidence or motivation to move from a 4 to a 5," is another way to get the client to think about what he or she needs to increase motivation. These techniques encourage the client to identify values and goals for behavior change and to resolve any ambivalence about changing.

The case manager's role during this process is to be empathic, avoiding judgments and arguments. It is also important for the case manager to articulate discrepancies between the client's words, behaviors, and goals and to direct the client's attention to an exploration of these discrepancies: "You say you want to quit smoking yet you keep a pack of cigarettes in your car. Tell me about that." Using the client's own words makes an impact on the client and prompts the client's recognition and exploration of the discrepancy. Any resistance or reluctance is a natural part of change and is met with "It is up to you" or "What you do is really your decision."

This brief overview of motivational interviewing enables you to see how it uses client strengths and client participation in changing. It differs from the traditional approaches or interventions that begin with problem identification, end with resolution, and involve confronting clients or persuading them that they must change. Often, these approaches actually increase resistance.

Summary

The strengths-based approach differs from older models that are problem-based or deficit-based assessments, followed by planning and implementation that target the problem(s). These older models have less client engagement and participation, are often provider driven, and focus on negative events or characteristics. They may actually lessen the client's ability to solve his or her own problems and encourage dependency on the case manager to define problems and identify strategies to resolve the problem. Older models and strengths-based approaches attempt to match clients and resources. The strengths-based approach also helps clients become their own case managers, assuming responsibility for themselves and their problems and motivating them to act in their own best interests.

·············● Exercise 7: Using the Strengths-Based Approach

Think about a change *you* would like to make. Identify the problem that you would like to address and complete the form (Figure 3) that follows.

FIGURE 3

Problem _____

Your Strengths	Your Resources	Barriers

What would you say to yourself to apply motivational interviewing?

_____

_____

_____

_____

 # Case Study

The following case introduces Joe, a homeless male. A brief case summary describes his current status.*

Case Management Service Plan: Homeless Adult

Homeless Joe, a 55-year-old male, SS# 555-55-5555, Axis I: Schizophrenia, Paranoid, 295.30; Alcohol Abuse, 305.0; Axis II: deferred, 799.9; Axis III: Anemia; Axis IV: problems with social environment, occupational problems, housing problems, economic problems, other psychosocial and environmental problems; Axis V: GAF at time of admission to CM, 40. Joe is a Vietnam veteran. While in the military, he was a radio operator, then a paramedic on the front line. He was honorably discharged in 1969. He completed two years of college before being drafted. He grew up in a small, lower-income community outside of a larger town. He has an older brother, but has little to no contact. A social worker (SW) at the regional mental health facility had seen Joe in the neighborhood where she lives, walking to and from town for many months. A year ago, the SW saw Joe walking home in the snow late one night and gave him a ride. She gave him a ride several times after that. At that time Joe was working nights at a dialysis clinic. Several months later, the SW saw Joe almost daily sitting in a field in the neighborhood. Some mornings it was evident Joe had spent the night sleeping in the field. The SW had often seen Joe purchase beer and snack food in the grocery. Joe had been arrested several times in the winter for intoxication. Recently the SW saw Joe living in a tent at the end of a dead-end street behind the grocery store. He usually appeared clean and in neat clothes but occasionally was wet and dirty. Attempts to talk with Joe indicated he was experiencing visual and auditory hallucinations and was very paranoid about his environment. He was guarded and anxious when engaged in conversation. He did state he occasionally worked mowing and doing yard work for a man who lives near his "tent house." Joe indicated he liked living outdoors and did not like confined settings. Joe was admitted to the regional mental health hospital in January, intoxicated and responding to internal stimuli. While in the hospital, he was referred for CM services. At the initial interview, he refused CM services. The SW, who had met Joe in the community, became aware of Joe's reluctance and, with the CM, visited Joe twice a week during his inpatient stay. When he was ready for discharge, he had agreed to CM services, but he was fearful of coming into the clinic for medication. He discharged on a x1 month Haldol Dec. He has met with his CM at his tent three times. They have talked about Joe's mental illness, his history, and what he would like to work on with the CM. It does not appear that Joe has had any prior mental health services, except for brief stays in the Veterans' hospital in 1970, 1989, and 1995. He has not taken any medication, other than while in the hospital. He drinks beer "when the voices are too loud." He has lived transiently, except for brief stays with family or in missions in three different states. His only income is from doing yard work and odd jobs when he can get them. He says he is tired of moving around and wants to stay in his home community. Today, the CM wants to talk with Joe about his service plan.

Exercise 8: Homeless Joe

1. You are meeting with Joe to talk about a service plan. How might you focus on strengths to engage Joe in case management?

_____

_____

_____

_____

_____

2. Describe how you would use motivational interviewing to help Joe change his present situation.

_____

_____

_____

Source: Material adapted from personal communication from Debby Lovin-Buuck, 2004.

....

THE STRENGTHS/RESOURCES ASSESSMENT IN THE SEVEN DOMAINS ✦ "HOMELESS JOE"

Case Manager: LaKeisha Day		Diagnosis Codes: Axis I: 295.30 Axis II: 799.9	Annual Plan Date: 8-14-03
SSN#: 555-55-5555		DOB: 6/8/xx	Sex: M

Presenting/Current Problem(s) : "Homeless Joe" is a 55 y/o male with a history of paranoid schizophrenia and alcohol abuse.

He is currently homeless and suffers from anemia. He has financial and occupational problems and little family support. Joe is experiencing daily auditory and visual hallucinations. He presents as guarded and anxious. He was admitted to the RMHI on August 3 on an involuntary basis. He refused case management (CM) in the past, but has now agreed to CM with Comprehensive Community Care (CCC).

Joe has not followed treatment recommendations, from the VA Hospital, for mediation management. His pattern has been to manage his mental illness with alcohol.

Domain Code:	Member Preferences:	Domain Code	Member Needs:
1–Living Arrangements	To live in his own apartment		Income, through employment &/or SSD
2–Leisure/Recreational	To hike in the mountains		Transportation, a hiking "buddy"
3–Vocational/ Educational	Part-time work, complete vocational classes		Referral to Vocational Rehab program or Technical Training program
4–Health/Medical	Learn to eat healthy foods; medical exam		PCP assignment and appointment
5–Social Support	No preferences at this time		At later time, phase into Links Program to increase socialization
6–Emotional/Behavioral	To learn to manage mental illness		Medication management skills
7–Financial	To have a monthly income		Apply for disability and vocational training

Member Strengths: Has lived in own apartment in the past. Can read. Knows how to shop. Has completed 2 years of college. Prior training as a paramedic while in the military. Was social, outgoing and had friends in high school. Has a desire for change. Has been working part time in lawn maintenance.	**Member Disadvantages:** Currently socially isolative, prefers living in his tent in the woods. No income. Poor health.

Signatures

Member	Date:	Case Manager	Date:
Psychiatrist	Date:	Mental Health Professional	Date:

Source: Debby Lovin-Buuck, LCSW, personal communication, December 12, 2004.

3. By focusing on strengths, what would you hope to accomplish in each of the three case management phases?

_____

_____

_____

_____

_____

4. What additional information would you like to have about Joe that would facilitate a strengths-based approach?

_____

_____

_____

_____

_____

5. What resources do you think are available for Joe? How would you find out?

_____

_____

_____

_____

_____

.... Self-Assessment

The following activity will help you assess what you have learned from Chapter 1. Focus on what you understand and what additional information would help you expand your knowledge about case management and its phases.

1. How will knowledge about the strengths-based approach influence your work as a case manager?

_____

_____

_____

2. Select one client from your text or one of the websites and describe how you would use motivational interviewing to begin case management.

_____

_____

_____

3. List the questions that remain for you after reading Chapter 1 in *Generalist Case Management* and the workbook.

_____

_____

_____

Pretest Answers

1. Assessment, planning, and implementation
2. (a) Professionals do not want to think about "clients" as cases. It is dehumanizing. (p. 4)
   (b) Clients do not want to be managed. (p. 4)
   (c) Helpers believe that they do more than manage cases. (p. 4)
3. There is an initial assessment of Roy's status: basic demographic information, information about medical history, educational history, social history, as well as other information about the client's reasons for seeking services. Basic information is used to begin to determine eligibility (pp. 7–12).
4. The basic purpose of the assessment phase is to gather information. This is guided by the purpose of the agency, the client's presenting problems, and other issues that the helper identifies. During the planning phase this is a reassessment to determine if any circumstances have changed for the client (pp. 7–12 and pp. 16–20).
5. How does a recipient of services participate in each of the three phases of case management?

   Assessment—the recipient of services provides basic information during the intake interview; helps define the presenting problems, and works with the helper to establish goals (p. 12).

   Planning—helper and client determine a service plan and together arrange for service delivery. Both participate in determining desired outcomes, suggesting services, and defining a successful intervention (pp. 16–18).

   Implementation—client provides feedback about services received, informs the helper if any changes in circumstances occur, and helps evaluate the case management process (p. 20).

 ## References

McQuaide, S., & Ehrenreich, J. H. (1997). Assessing client strengths. *Families in Society*, 78 (2), 201–212.

Saleeby, D. (1997). *The strengths perspective in social work practice*. White Plains, NY: Longman.

Van Wormer, K., & Davis, D. R. (2003). *Addiction treatment: A strengths perspective*. Pacific Grove, CA: Brooks/Cole/Thomson.

Chapter 2

Historical Perspectives of Case Management

Chapter 2 in *Generalist Case Management* explores the foundations of case management and the influence of institutions, organizations, legislation, and managed care on its development. The following exercises enable you to further develop your case management knowledge and skills.

 **Pretest**

When you finish reading Chapter 2 in *Generalist Case Management,* answer the following questions and complete the items.

1. How has the role of the case manager evolved from the 1970s to the present?

_____

_____

_____

_____

_____

2. List the historical contributions of individual and organizational pioneers to case management as a service delivery strategy.

_____

_____

_____

_____

_____

3. How has federal legislation since 1970 contributed to the evolution of case management?

_____

_____

_____

_____

_____

4. Describe the three types of managed care organizations.

_____

_____

_____

_____

_____

5. What has been the impact of managed care on case management and service delivery?

_____

_____

_____

_____

_____

6. Complete the crossword puzzle as a way to review the history of case management introduced in Chapter 2 of *Generalist Case Management* text.

Across

1 Mary Richmond developed social ___.
3 Older Americans Act advanced case management by recognizing the need to ___ care.
5 Health insurance program for ages 65 and older.
6 Establishes contracts with providers allowing better benefits for services provided.
8 Federal disability insurance program.
9 Focus of the Older Americans Act of 1965 was to provide services in order to improve ___.
12 Responsibility to authorize or deny services to ensure efficient use of resources.
13 A measurement of the cost and efficiency of services.
15 Changes in job titles reflect the ___ of case management and service delivery.
16 Developed Social Diagnosis.
17 Founder of the Massachusetts School of Idiotic and Feebleminded Youth.
18 Organizational structure that allows a variety of payment plans but restricts clients' access to providers.
19 Case management takes place in a group home or a ___.

Down

1 Moving people from institutions to community-based settings.
2 Provides monthly cash to eligible low-income persons with limited resources.
4 The emphasis of modern case management is client ___.
5 Largest insurance program providing medical care to low-income individuals.
7 Structure that combines health service delivery and financing.
10 A key element for successful case management.
11 Use of a casework approach to assist individuals began during this.
14 Neighborhood center started by Jane Addams and Ellen Starr.

Chapter Summary

Foundations of case management include the work of early pioneers in helping professions, new organizations and institutions, and federal legislation. Beginning in the late 1800s, institutional settings, such as the Massachusetts School of Idiotic and Feebleminded Youth, were established to provide services and support to individuals with cognitive, physical, or developmental disabilities. During the early part of the twentieth century, the American Red Cross and Departments of Public Health each contributed significantly to the field of case management. For example, the American Red Cross used a casework approach as early as 1911, during the Mexican civil war. During the 1960s, several federal legislative efforts recognized the need for social services. One example is the Older Americans Act of 1965 that mandated case management as one component of services provided.

During the 1980s, our society witnessed the development of managed care. With this new model of health care came an increased need for case managers. Three models of managed care have emerged in an attempt to maintain cost and ensure quality of service delivery. The Health Maintenance Organization (HMO) combines service delivery and financing into one system. The second model of managed care, the Preferred Provider Organization (PPO), allows a little more flexibility for consumers by allowing service delivery outside of the network but with fewer benefits. The third option in managed care is the Point-of-Service (POS) plan. The POS plan also offers flexibility to the consumer, but requires higher premiums, deductibles, and percentages of medical fees from the consumer. Managed care has advantages and disadvantages, and advocacy efforts, such as the patient bill of rights developed by the American Psychological Association, have evolved in response to frustrations with managed care.

The following exercises provide opportunities for you to think about the history and development of case management.

Exercise 1: Modern-Day Case Management

Remember Bobby, the case manager you met in Chapter 1. Go to www.thomsonedu.com/counseling/mcclam, Chapter 2, Link 1, to hear Bobby talk about the differences between traditional case management and modern-day case management. Answer the following questions.

1. How does Bobby define traditional case management?

_____

_____

_____

_____

2. How does Bobby's understanding of traditional case management compare with case management described in Chapter 2?

_____

_____

_____

_____

3. How does Bobby's understanding of modern-day case management compare with the description of case management today described in the text?

_____

_____

_____

_____

·············● **Exercise 2: The Influence of Mary Richmond**

Denise Dedman has collected quotes from Mary Richmond's 1922 work, *What is Social Case Work?* The quotes range from a description of case records to a definition of casework and advice for providing individualized treatment. The following information comes directly from her web page, http://www.westshore.edu/personal/dededman/PAGE8.HTMl:

· · · · · · · · ·

✦ **A Brief Biographical Sketch…**

Mary Ellen Richmond was one of the women who influenced the direction of the social work profession in its very beginning. She was born to Henry and Lavinia Richmond on August 5, 1861 in Belleville, Illinois, and was the only one of their children to survive infancy. At the age of three her mother died and she was sent to live with her grandmother and two aunts. In 1878 she graduated from Baltimore Eastern Female High School. Richmond cared for one of her aunts until her death. In 1888 she began to work for the Baltimore Charity Organization Society. By 1897 she was advocating the establishment of professional schools for the study of casework. She wrote several books including Social Diagnosis *and* What is Social Case Work? *Here are some quotes from that text.*

*What Is Social Case Work?** Written by Mary E. Richmond, 1922.

On Case Records

"At first their attempts were little more than a rambling chronicle of motions made in the course of their work, but gradually they learned to construct good, chronological accounts both of the essential processes used and of the observations upon which these processes were based. A record so made becomes not only an indispensable guide to future action on behalf of the person recorded; it can be unexcelled material for training other caseworkers."

Definition of Case Work

"Social case work consists of those processes which develop personality through adjustments consciously effected, individual by individual, between men and their social environment. The treatment items classified in my list under direct action begin with those services, often of the humblest sort, which tend to strengthen personal relations with a client."

On Change

"The human mind is not a fixed and unalterable thing. . . . On the contrary it is a living, growing, changing, highly suggestible thing, capable of receiving strong impressions from without, of forming new habits, of responding to opportunity, of assimilating the good as well as the bad."

On Human Frailty

"There is no such thing as a 'self-made man,' and the phrase, once so popular, has fallen into disuse. It may happen to any one of us at any time and has already happened to every one of us more than once, to fall out of adjustment with our world through some failure to meet our opportunities, some temporary shock from without, or through irreparable loss."

On the Uniqueness of Each Individual

"If we agreed that the state exists for the highest good of its members, we must also agree that there is no lesson democracy needs to take more to heart than this lesson in sound administration; namely, Treat unequal things unequally."

Source: Richmond, Mary Ellen. From *What Is Social Case Work? An Introductory Description.* © Russell Sage Foundation, 112 East 64th Street, New York, NY 10021. Reprinted with permission.

On Client Self-Determination

"One test of any social treatment is the degree to which all the persons involved in it have been able, to the limit of their ability, to take an active part in achieving the desired result."

On Individualized Treatment

"A sense of frustration cannot be overcome by cheerful and vague general advice. For this type of social treatment it is necessary for a worker to learn the art of discovering the major interests of the individual, and of utilizing them to reknit a broken connection or supply a motive lacking before."

On School Social Work (Visiting Teachers)

"It is still difficult however for the community to realize that the problems of the school are not wholly educational, that they are, in part, social. (The visiting teacher) undertakes, for a given number of pupils reported to her by the school for poor scholarship, bad health, misconduct, lateness, irregular attendance, or for what appear to be adverse home conditions, to discover the causal factors in the difficulty then tries to work out a better adjustment. The measures she employs are the exercising of personal influence, winning the cooperation of parents, seeking the advice and assistance of medical and mental experts, seeking the aid of various social agencies, utilizing various recreational facilities, and changing the child's environment."

As you think about each of these quotes, discuss each in terms of the influences Mary Richmond had on case management.

1. On Case Records

_____

_____

_____

_____

2. Definition of Case Work

_____

_____

_____

_____

3. On Change

_____

_____

_____

_____

4. On Human Frailty

_____

_____

_____

_____

5. On the Uniqueness of Each Individual

_____

_____

_____

_____

6. On Client Self-Determination

_____

_____

_____

_____

7. On Individualized Treatment

_____

_____

_____

_____

8. On School Social Work (Visiting Teachers)

_____

_____

_____

_____

 # Exercise 3: Legislation and Case Management

Congress passed the Rehabilitation Act of 1973 in an effort to provide for each American with physical and mental disabilities support to "live independently, enjoy self-determination, make choices, contribute to society, pursue meaningful careers, and enjoy full inclusion and integration in the economic, political, social, cultural, and educational mainstream of American society" (Rehabilitation Services Administration, 2003). The Act contained five themes:

- ✦ Serve individuals with severe disabilities
- ✦ Encourage consumer involvement
- ✦ Conduct rigorous evaluation
- ✦ Support research
- ✦ Advocate for the rights of the disabled (Region 8 Rehabilitation Continuing Education Programs, 2002)

The two terms, *assessment* and *community rehabilitation program,* are of particular interest to the case manager working with the rehabilitation client. The description of assessment, as it relates to serving the rehabilitation client, is used to determine eligibility and define the vocational rehabilitation needs of the client. The definition of a community rehabilitation program describes the broad responsibilities of the program and the wide variety of services offered. The following is taken directly from the Rehabilitation Act of 1973, Section 7, Numbers 2 and 5:

(2) Assessment for determining eligibility and vocational rehabilitation needs

The term "assessment for determining eligibility and vocational rehabilitation needs" means, as appropriate in each case—

(A)(i) a review of existing data—

(I) to determine whether an individual is eligible for vocational rehabilitation services; and
(II) to assign priority for an order of selection described in section 101(a)(5)(A) in the States that use an order of selection pursuant to section 101(a)(5)(A); and

(ii) to the extent necessary, the provision of appropriate assessment activities to obtain necessary additional data to make such determination and assignment;

(B) to the extent additional data is necessary to make a determination of the employment outcomes, and the nature and scope of vocational rehabilitation services, to be included in the individualized plan for employment of an eligible individual, a comprehensive assessment to determine the unique strengths, resources, priorities, concerns, abilities, capabilities, interests, and informed choice, including the need for supported employment, of the eligible individual, which comprehensive assessment—

(i) is limited to information that is necessary to identify the rehabilitation needs of the individual and to develop the individualized plan for employment of the eligible individual;

(ii) uses, as a primary source of such information, to the maximum extent possible and appropriate and in accordance with confidentiality requirements—

(I) existing information obtained for the purposes of determining the eligibility of the individual and assigning priority for an order of selection described in section 101(a)(5)(A) for the individual; and
(II) such information as can be provided by the individual and, where appropriate, by the family of the individual;
(iii) may include, to the degree needed to make such a determination, an assessment of the personality, interests, interpersonal skills, intelligence and related functional capacities, educational achievements, work experience, vocational aptitudes, personal and social adjustments, and employment opportunities of the individual, and the medical, psychiatric, psychological, and other pertinent vocational, educational, cultural, social, recreational, and environmental factors, that affect the employment and rehabilitation needs of the individual; and

(iv) may include, to the degree needed, an appraisal of the patterns of work behavior of the individual and services needed for the individual to acquire occupational skills, and to develop work attitudes, work habits, work tolerance, and social and behavior patterns necessary for successful job performance, including the utilization of work in real job situations to assess and develop the capacities of the individual to perform adequately in a work environment;

(C) referral, for the provision of rehabilitation technology services to the individual, to assess and develop the capacities of the individual to perform in a work environment; and

(D) an exploration of the individual's abilities, capabilities, and capacity to perform in work situations, which shall be assessed periodically during trial work experiences, including experiences in which the individual is provided appropriate supports and training

(5) Community rehabilitation program

The term "community rehabilitation program" means a program that provides directly or facilitates the provision of vocational rehabilitation services to individuals with disabilities, and that provides, singly or in combination, for an individual with a disability to enable the individual to maximize opportunities for employment, including career advancement—

(A) medical, psychiatric, psychological, social, and vocational services that are provided under one management;

(B) testing, fitting, or training in the use of prosthetic and orthotic devices;

(C) recreational therapy;

(D) physical and occupational therapy;

(E) speech, language, and hearing therapy;

(F) psychiatric, psychological, and social services, including positive behavior management;

(G) assessment for determining eligibility and vocational rehabilitation needs;

(H) rehabilitation technology;

(I) job development, placement, and retention services;

(J) evaluation or control of specific disabilities;

(K) orientation and mobility services for individuals who are blind;

(L) extended employment;

(M) psychosocial rehabilitation services;

(N) supported employment services and extended services;

(O) services to family members when necessary to the vocational rehabilitation of the individual;

(P) personal assistance services; or

(Q) services similar to the services described in one of subparagraphs (A) through (P)

Assume that you are one of the first case managers to work with rehabilitation clients based upon the Rehabilitation Act of 1973. Using the information provided, define your responsibilities as a rehabilitation case manager in terms of the following:

Job title:

_____

_____

Job description:

_____

_____

_____

_____

Primary responsibilities:

_____

_____

_____

_____

Record keeping:

_____

_____

_____

_____

Client involvement:

_____

_____

_____

_____

Exercise 4: Working in the Managed Care Environment

Managed care represents a model of health and mental health care delivery used in the United States today. Case managers, working for mental health agencies and organizations, must convince managed care professionals that their clients need the services provided under the guidelines and directions of a managed care organizations. For example, a client comes to an agency for treatment of depression. The agency or the client must have the managed care organization's approval before either private insurance or state insurance will pay for the mental health services. Managed care may also determine if the diagnosis is warranted, what the standard of care is for the diagnosis, and what the fee structure is for the services rendered.

What is it like to participate as a client in the managed care environment? Understanding the client perspective provides us one good way to appreciate case management within the context of managed care. The following experience of Kathy Rinehart, an adult suffering from manic depression, offers a glance into mental health care within the managed care context.

I'll Say I'm Suicidal

The Mentally Ill Struggle through the Maze of Managed Care

Kathy Rhinehart knew the routine. Voices in her head. Paranoia. She thought the television set was talking about her. The lyrics of a song—a Carly Simon tune, she thinks—took on personal and ominous meaning. A 15-year history of manic depression had taught her what to do when those symptoms hit. "I know when I need to be in the hospital," the Cedar Falls, Iowa, woman says.

But her insurer, one of the new managed care companies specializing in mental health, thought otherwise. Rhinehart spent several hours in a hospital waiting room talking to doctors, nurses, and clerks, who in turn talked to managed care representatives from Medco (since bought by Merit Behavioral Care Corp.), which administered her mental health benefits. Company officials eventually sent word back that she must go home. "I think they said it was because I wasn't suicidal," she says. But the voices got louder and more urgent, and she grew increasingly terrified. She returned to the hospital the next day, only to be turned away again. What had always worked—checking into a psychiatric unit for care and medication adjustment—wasn't working under the new managed care rules.

Within two days, she saw another way out. "I had all my pills. I got the glass of water. I was ready to take them," she says. But before she swallowed anything, her boyfriend came home and rushed her to the hospital, where she was admitted. Now, she's learned a new aspect of the routine: "Next time, I'll just say I'm suicidal, so I can get into the hospital."

If you were a mental health care coordinator for Kathy, describe how you would work with the managed care professionals supervising Kathy's care by completing the following items.

1. Describe Kathy's difficulties.

_____

_____

_____

_____

2. Write a rationale for the services Kathy needs.

_____

_____

_____

_____

3. Describe the consequences for Kathy if she does not receive services.

_____

_____

_____

_____

 # Exercise 5: Working with the Client in a Managed Care Environment

1. Study the description of Health Maintenance Organizations (HMOs), Preferred Provider Organizations (PPOs), and Point of Service (POSs) in Chapter 2 in *Generalist Case Management* and the definitions that follow to understand what each of the different types of managed care models offers to the client.

Definitions

PPO—Preferred Provider Organization. A network of physicians, hospitals, and other providers/services. The Blue Cross Blue Shield Tennessee Provider Network is a PPO. After meeting a yearly deductible, benefits are paid at a higher level for services received within the PPO network than if services are received outside the network.

HMO—Health Maintenance Organization. A managed health plan where all care is coordinated through a primary care physician. Most of the time, no benefits are paid for care received apart from the HMO's network. Typically, minimal co-payments, often $15 to $25, are paid each time service is received.

POS—Point of Service. A plan managed like an HMO with an option to receive care outside the plan's network. Care received through the POS network has HMO-level benefits. Outside the POS network, a deductible is required and benefits are paid at around 70 percent of UC.

(Definitions, 1996).

2. Read this example of Rosa and Paul Hernandez, who want you to make a recommendation about which managed care model they should use. They have been your clients for almost two years. Paul has been in the hospital for a heart bypass and gall bladder surgery. You coordinated his care plan

following the heart surgery. Rosa, in her late 20s, is worried about their health insurance. Although her husband seems healthy enough now, her family history includes early detection of breast cancer, heart disease, and diabetes. Under their current health insurance plan, they have paid more than $50,000 in medical bills over the last two years. They are thinking of changing their health plan and come asking for help.

a. As you think with them about their options, what points about each choice would you emphasize?

_____

_____

_____

_____

b. Which option do you believe is their best choice? Why?

_____

_____

_____

_____

In More Depth: Legislative Savvy

Most case managers are aware of the mission and goals of the agency or program for which they work. In addition, they understand their roles and responsibilities, the characteristics of the population they serve, and the policies and procedures they follow as they perform their jobs. Yet many of these helpers have a limited view or understanding of the broader perspective of the social legislation that undergirds the services they provide.

As described in Chapter 2, History of Case Management, a number of past and current federal legislative acts include case management in the guidelines for implementation. These assume that case management is the best practice for providing services to those in need. Case management services can also be mandated through state or local legislation.

Whether the source of the legislation is federal, state, or local, knowledge of legislation and the legislative process helps case managers more clearly understand the case management service that they are providing. Detailed knowledge of rules and regulations promulgated by governmental agencies furnishes background information to view policies, procedures, and paperwork in a different way. If the case manager understands the origins of legislation, it is easier to understand professional responsibility within a larger framework. This knowledge may help the case manager distinguish the practices that allow flexibility from those that are non-negotiable. Sometimes practices are clear cut and other times practices are less clear.

This situation describes how a legislative bill becomes a law and introduces guidelines on how to read a legislative bill. A look at the Office of the Assistant Secretary for Planning and Evaluation of the Department of Health and Human Services introduces a way case managers can become involved in or track the legislative process.

How a Bill Becomes a Law

A bill is proposed to change a statute, introduce a new law, or request appropriations. The following steps describe the journey of a bill through the legislative process.

Measure is introduced. Members of Congress introduce a bill drafted by themselves and other constituencies. Once the bill is introduced, it is given a number and referred to committee.

Measure referred to committee. The measure goes through a number of reviews and votes. There are opportunities for revision or amendments. What is passed may only vaguely resemble what was proposed.

Leadership schedules measure. Once the bill is sent to the House or Senate, it receives a date for consideration and debate. If the bill passes in one legislative chamber, it is sent to the other chamber.

Joint consideration. The House and Senate agree on the legislation with amendments and appoint members to a conference committee. This committee reconciles differences and prepares a conference report.

Presidential action. The President may sign the bill, and it becomes law. The President may also veto the bill. If the President does not sign the bill, but does not veto it, after ten days, the bill becomes law.

How to Read Legislation

Legislative bills are complex documents that describe the intent and scope of that law and indicate how the law is to be implemented. The following guidelines are useful to learn about legislation.

1. *Review the short title of the act in Section 1.* This provides you with the focus of the law. For example, Public Law 104-193, Section 1, "This act may be cited as the 'Personal Responsibility and Work Opportunity Reconciliation Act of 1996' (PRWORA) (Public Law 104-193 [August 22, 1996]. 110 Stat. 2105, 104th Congress. Retrieved September 8, 2005, from http://wdr.doleta.gov/readroom/legislation/pdf/104-193.pdf).
2. *Review the table of contents.* It lists "Titles" or areas that elaborate on the scope and implementation of the act. The entries in the table of contents indicate the scope of the act. For example, the Titles of PRWORA include:

   ✦ Title I Block Grants for Temporary Assistance for Needy Families
   ✦ Title II Supplemental Security Income
   ✦ Title III Child Support
   ✦ Title IV Restricting Welfare and Public Benefits for Aliens
   ✦ Title V Child Protection
   ✦ Title VI Child Care
   ✦ Title VII Child Nutrition Programs.

3. *Review the rationale for each Title included in the act.* The rationale provides the intent and the scope of that component of the act. It also provides data and rationale for the inclusion of that Title in the legislation. Often the rationale for the act is included in many of the early Titles. For example, Title I Block Grants for Temporary Assistance for Needy Families details from Congressional hearings such as the importance of marriage in a successful society.
4. *Study the role of the states or the local government in implementing the act.* This component of the legislation helps case managers understand the specific responsibilities each level of government must assume and allows case managers to distinguish among federal, state, and local guidelines. For example, PRWORA outlines the scope and intent of the act, but gives individual states the responsibility of determining how they will address the needs of the families requiring assistance. According to the public law, "The purpose of this part [of the act] is to increase the flexibility of the states operating a program" (Public Law 104-193 [August 22, 1996]. 110 Stat. 2105, 104th Congress. Retrieved September 8, 2005, from http://wdr.doleta.gov/readroom/legislation/pdf/104-193.pdf) The states were given deadlines for submitting their plans that included how the programs would assist families, engage adults in work, reduce out-of-wedlock pregnancies, as well as other areas of focus.

Office of Program Systems: Tracking Legislative Development

There is an additional way in which case managers can learn about the legislative process related to the more than 300 health and social services programs under the jurisdiction of the Department of Health and Human Services (DHHS). The department's Office of the Assistant Secretary for Planning and Evaluation (ASPE) maintains a website (http://aspe.hhs.gov/progsys/legi/legi.htm) that describes the legislation DHHS is developing. To involve an integrated team of people to review budget, legal counsel, policy, and programs, ASPE conducts a full review of proposals before recommending they be sent to Congress. This website also contains guidelines for citizen-developed proposals as well other legislative links. This is an excellent site for case managers to seek current information about legislation.

Now let's look at how federal and state legislation affects the work of one case manager, Casey Rusk. Casey works with parents and children receiving support from PRWORA. She describes her responsibilities and frustrations linked to changing federal and state guidelines that govern the policies and procedures of her program.

● Casey Rusk: Case Manager for Families Help

Prelude

Under the PRWORA mandates, each state must develop guidelines for and implement a plan to deliver support to families through TANF Block grants. Casey Rusk works for Families Help, a program developed by her state to serve families in need of support. Her supervisor, Jorge Linkus, has just received a copy of an evaluation of the Families Help program completed by 75 percent of the case managers in the state. The report uncovered a serious dissatisfaction on the part of these professionals. Linkus feels if he has a firsthand account of what it is like to be a case manager in his program, then he can use the information to make changes at the local level. He recognizes that many of the complaints reflect mandates from the federal and state government. Nonetheless, he wants to try to support the case managers in his office. Linkus asks Rusk to provide him a detailed account of some of the difficulties that she encounters in her job. Rusk supplies some background information about her work at Families Help and shares with us the report that she has written for her supervisor.

Working as a Case Manager at the Department of Human Services: Families Help Program

---

My name is Casey. I live in the Midwest and have been working for the Families Help program for about four years. In my department there are 15 case managers; I started the job because three of my best friends worked here. Right now there are two women who have been case managers for over five years. I am third in terms of seniority; the remaining case managers are relatively new. Each year we have at least three case managers leave the Families Help program for other jobs.

I have been thinking about my work ever since January when I filled out a survey about my experience at the Department of Human Services: why I stay, how long I expect to stay, why I would want to leave, what my skills are, and how I would like to be trained. Let me tell you a little about the work that I do.

Right now my major responsibility is as a case manager for families who are eligible for TANF support in the Families Help program. This is the old welfare program. Although I never worked for the welfare system, I still hear clients and staff refer to our program as welfare. Being a case manager means that I help establish client eligibility for the program, help clients develop a plan for gaining employment within a limited time period, coordinate the services the clients receive, follow up on client progress, and maintain a record of the services provided and the outcomes achieved. Although it has been an exciting time to work in our program, it has also been a time of stress. I believe that very few individuals actually have an understanding of what we do. Maybe that is why there are so many changes. Over the past four years, my job description and responsibilities as a case manager have shifted.

Yesterday my boss, Mr. Linkus asked me and another case manager who has been working for the Families Help program for six months to look at the report of the state survey of case managers. He wants me to respond to six questions that he considers important, expanding upon my thoughts beyond the information provided on the survey. He explained that information we provide him will give him a better understanding of the issues and challenges we face. I spent three days working on this document. I hope my comments will help case managers in our department and the families we work with.

> TO: *Jorge Linkus*
> FROM: *Casey Rusk*
>
> SUBJECT: *Survey Report*

1. *How long have you worked at DHS?*

   I have worked for DHS for four years. During that time, even though I have not changed jobs, I have had various responsibilities.

2. *How long do you expect to work here?*

   I do not expect to be working for DHS in five years.

3. *Why will you be/not be working for DHS in 5 years?*

The primary reason that I want to change jobs is because the work is so stressful. I am also constantly off balance in this job for three reasons: There are too many changes; there is little support for us case managers when we need it; and my caseload is too large to handle. There is just too much work. Here are the types of changes that I have experienced during my time with the Families Help program.

The first change was in the actual responsibilities I have. When I first came to work here, all 15 of us were case managers, but we worked in teams of 3 managers each; each team had a different responsibility. A team of 3 that performed the intake with clients. Even though many of the clients had been in the old welfare program, all clients had to reapply based upon a new set of requirements. Other teams established eligibility, developed Families Help case management plans, coordinated services, or evaluated services. To prepare for these responsibilities we all traveled to the state office for training. The early difficulties included having limited knowledge about each of our clients, having trouble getting policy and procedure questions answered, and not being able to respond to questions that our clients had. We all tried to read the state manual. Sometimes the state referred us to the federal manual. Often neither made sense to us.

My job as a case manager has been through two sets of changes since then, but I have no idea why any of the changes were made. When I first came, I was an intake case manager. Each day I came to the office, saw clients, asked them questions, and passed that information along to the eligibility case manager. Our team of intake workers met once a month to talk together. During a period of nine months our intake forms changed twice. We heard it was because we needed additional information for the state and the federal government.

My second job was as an eligibility case manager. I did not receive any training except on the job training. The co-workers on my team helped me understand how to establish eligibility for our families. Since much of the information we used came from the intake form, I had a deeper appreciation for the intake process.

The third change was taking all 15 case manager positions and revising them. Each case manager was given a caseload and was expected to perform all of the responsibilities previously provided by each of the five teams. In other words, I am performing intake, establishing eligibility, developing Families Help case management plans, coordinating services, and evaluating services. The transition was almost impossible since many of us had only the knowledge and skills to perform one of our jobs. Unfortunately, because the state was under financial pressure, there was no centralized training. We tried to train each other. I do like this change because I know my clients better. But, I still feel unprepared to document outcomes. That is my weakest skill. And of course I have too many clients and am not able to work with them in the way that might really help them.

Another difficulty that I face as a case manager is understanding how our program integrates with other government programs. For example, in 2000, a Victims of Trafficking and Violence Protection Act (Public Law 106-38) passed to provide certain benefits to victims who have been forced into prostitution, slavery, or forced labor. The bottom line of that law is that these victims are eligible for TANF funds. Establishing this eligibility is complicated. Here is another example. In 2003 there was a push for Child Support personnel and TANF case managers to work together to help clients supplement their income with child support from the noncustodial parent (Department of Health and Human Services, Administration for Children and Families, 2003). One set of clients whose eligibility is in question is immigrants who are victims of domestic violence. According to federal policy, some battered immigrants meet criteria for eligibility while others do not (Office for Civil Rights, 2005). These are just two examples of the complicated circumstances we deal with and that add considerable work to the case management process.

I want to emphasize that we have had little training to do what we do. Each time there is a change, I read the manual and the instructions from the federal and state government to try to figure out why the computer screens have changed, how I am to find out answers to the questions, and how I can help my clients. Too many times we are told to do something one way and then asked why did you do it that way.

I don't want to be too negative. I enjoy my work, and I feel like I am helping others. I also want to mention that although I am single now, I expect to be married within the next two years and I would like to begin a family. I know that I will still have to work, but I believe that this pay will not allow me to provide for my family.

4. *What is your level of comfort with your expertise in your primary job area(s)?*

The major difficulty for me that I have already talked about is the lack of training. We need more and much of the training is inadequate. I know that things keep changing as we respond to government requests, but if we want to do a good job, well we need to know what we are doing. And sometimes I am overwhelmed because of the complexities of the job. I am not an expert at anything except intake and eligibility.

I think that the main difficulty is PRWORA forces changes in the way we work. And the change is constant. It would be great if we could have training as the changes are made.

5. *How would you like to be trained?*

My favorite way to learn is with the teacher in front. I think that most of my co-workers agree. I really like to have a live teacher so I can ask questions and I can ask them more than once if I need to.

It is clear from Casey's report that she is committed to the goals of her department, or at least she is committed to the goals that she understands. But she does not believe that her work environment supports her efforts. She also thinks that the federal and state governments do not provide a stable environment from which she can do her job. She is frustrated with lack of support, too many changes, and a limited view of her part in the larger welfare reform program.

Exercise 6: Understanding Legislation

Assume that you are also a case manager in Casey Rusk's office and you have decided to expand your knowledge about PRWORA.

1. Outline the information you would seek from the Internet.

_____

_____

_____

_____

2. Provide a list of three useful Internet sites that you found, describe each site, and explain how this knowledge will help you perform your job more effectively.

Site 1:

_____

_____

_____

_____

Site 2:

_____

_____

_____

_____

Site 3:

_____

_____

_____

_____

··············● Self-Assessment

The following activity will help you assess what you have learned in Chapter 2. As you conclude your study of this chapter, answer the following questions. Focus on what you understand and what additional information can help you as you expand your knowledge about case management.

1. List and describe or define three concepts that contribute to your understanding of case management.

_____

_____

_____

_____

2. Select one client from the text or from the workbook and discuss how the concepts you list and define in Item 1 influence how you would work with that client.

_____

_____

_____

_____

3. List the questions that remain for you after reading Chapter 2 in the text and the workbook.

_____

_____

_____

_____

··············● Pretest Answers

1. Role of case manager: began with deinstitutionalization (p. 32), evolved from manager to coordinator/liaison (p. 37), expanded client involvement (p. 35), began to include providing diverse service delivery and a broader range of responsibilities (p. 37), and emphasized a more efficient use of resources (p. 38).
2. Historical contributions: The Massachusetts School tracked client progress, provided aftercare, and began an information management system (p. 39). The Hull House services included confidential record keeping and an emphasis on advocacy (p. 40). Henry Street Settlement House services included a visiting nurse providing the foundation for the American Red Cross (p. 42), and Mary Richmond introduced the concept of social diagnosis (p. 42).
3. Federal legislation: Older Americans Act emphasized multiplicity of human needs (p. 44); Rehabilitation Act of 1973 promoted consumer involvement (p. 48); the Family Support Act of 1988 and the Personal Responsibility and Work Opportunity Act provided new status for case manager (p. 49).
4. Three types of managed care organizations: HMOs are a combination of delivery and financing (p. 51). PPOs have contracts with preferred providers and benefits (p. 52), and POSs have higher fees, reduced coverage, and more flexibility (p. 52).
5. Impact of managed care: increased demand for case management; new models (p. 50); definitions of service delivery (p. 50).
6. See Crossword Puzzle Answers.

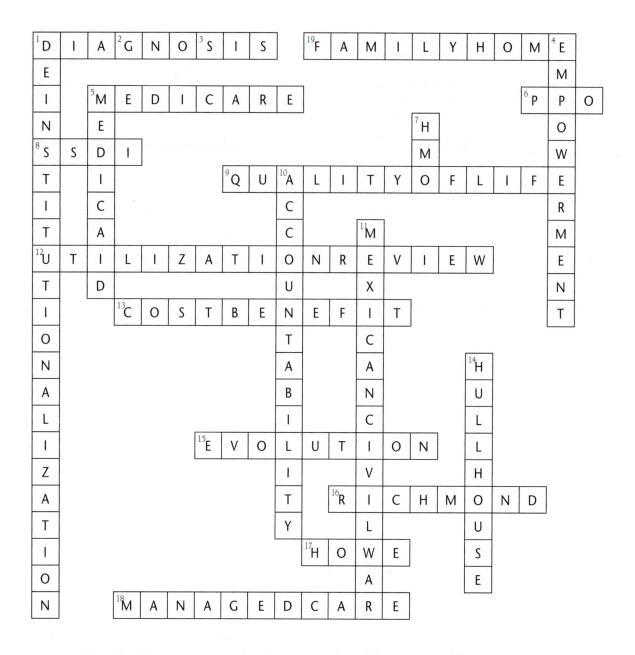

••••••••••••• 🔵 **References**

Brink, S. (1998, January 19). I'll Say I'm Suicidal. *U.S. News and World Report,* 63–64, 66.

Dedman, D. (n.d.). Introduction to Social Work (n.d.). Mary Richmond. Retrieved June 1, 2003, from http://home.westshore.cc.mi.us/dededman/PAGE8.HTML

Definitions. (1996, December). *Your Health Networker,* 4(4), 1.

Region 8 Rehabilitation Continuing Education Programs (2002). Module One. Retrieved June 2, 2003, from http://www.region8recep.com.

Rehabilitation History and Legislation Rehabilitation Continuing Education Programs. Retrieved February 7, 2003, from Programs http://www.unco.edu/rrcep/pdf/module%20one.pdf.

Rehabilitation Services Administration. (n.d.). The Rehabilitation Act of 1973 (n.d.). Retrieved February 7, 2003, from www.ed.gov/offices/OSERS/RSA/Policy/Legislation/rehabact.doc.

Chapter 3

Models of Case Management

Chapter 3 in *Generalist Case Management* shapes the context of case management by identifying the roles a case manager may assume and introducing three models within which case management might occur. The diverse roles and models illustrate the flexibility of the case management process. The following chapter furnishes opportunities for you to apply what you have learned about case management roles and models.

 **Pretest**

After reading Chapter 3 in *Generalist Case Management*, answer the following questions and complete the items.

1. Often a case manager must assume a number of different roles to meet client needs. Ideally, roles are determined by the goals for service delivery that the client and case manager establish. For each of the following goals, identify two roles you would assume and state your purpose in assuming each role.

   ◆ A case manager and an 18-year-old substance abuser agree that the client will quit using crack.

   _____

   _____

   _____

   _____

   ◆ A case manager and a 45-year-old parolee plan prison aftercare.

   _____

   _____

   _____

   _____

   ◆ A case manager and a pregnant teen plan care for her new baby.

   _____

   _____

   _____

   _____

   ◆ A case manager, a teacher, and a middle-school student plan in-school suspension.

   _____

   _____

   _____

   _____

   ◆ A case manager and 22-year-old twin sisters plan for life after the death of their mother in an automobile accident.

   _____

   _____

   _____

   _____

✦ A case manager works with a daughter whose mother resides in a nursing home. The mother needs more intensive care.

_____

_____

_____

_____

2. What are the specific goals of role-based, organization-based, and responsibility-based case management?

Role
based: _____

_____

Organization
based: _____

_____

Responsibility
based: _____

_____

3. One of your grandfathers can no longer take care of himself. What model of case management would you choose to provide services? What are the strengths of this model for your grandfather's situation?

_____

_____

_____

_____

● Chapter Summary

The model of case management that an agency uses often determines the ways in which case managers deliver services. In our society, there are three models of case management: role-based, organization-based, and responsibility-based case management. The case manager should be aware of these models, the way in which services are provided, their similarities and differences, and their strengths and weaknesses. In role-based case management, the case manager might act as a single point of access for the client and assume a variety of roles as needed. In organization-based case management, the case manager may also act as a single point of access for the client, but this model differs from role-based case management in that all of the services are available in one location. In the third model, responsibility-based case management, the focus is on the transition of care from human service professionals to nonprofessionals.

In each model of case management, a case manager might assume a number of roles. The work of case managers is often a function of the role they play in service delivery. For example, a case manager who is working as an "advocate" for his or her clients will often speak on behalf of clients, address issues of inequality and discrimination, work to influence government policy, or serve as a community organizer. The actual work of a case manager as an advocate would be very different from that of a case manager as a counselor. Other roles that case managers commonly assume include broker, coordinator, consultant, planner, problem solver, and record keeper. Many times, a case manager may function primarily in one role but engage in other roles as needed.

············● **Exercise 1: Roles and Models**

The following seven examples present case management services in different areas of the United States. Identify the model described and a minimum of two roles that will be necessary.

NEW YORK CITY: Third Avenue Family Services provides case management to families, especially those with children. Families must apply for services at the Third Avenue office. Intake information is gathered so eligibility can be determined. Services available include educational classes for mothers, child care, food and clothing donations, and one-night temporary housing.

Model: _____

Roles: _____

ST. LOUIS, MO: Marion Hall Emergency Shelter houses young women who have run away from home. They are placed in the shelter from two weeks to 30 days. During that time the young women are housed and fed and given educational and psychological assistance. Many clients "run" after they have been placed at Marion Hall. They resent the supervision and want to be on their own.

Model: _____

Roles: _____

LOS ANGELES: Intensive Case Management Program serves persistently mentally ill clients, people who have needs that can't be met in two or three months. Case managers "do what it takes" to help their clients. The goal is for clients to live in the community. They teach clients daily living skills and provide transportation, mental health care, recreation, and other services.

Model: _____

Roles: _____

LOS ANGELES: At Roosevelt High School, case managers assist the school with identifying their resources and helping them link with community resources. There is a student health and human service action team, where the school and the community come together. The case manager makes sure that each student receives the services needed. For example, if a teen is pregnant, that teen receives post-pregnancy planning and health and mental health care. Ultimately, the parents and the teens themselves assume the case management responsibility.

Model: _____

Roles: _____

ST. LOUIS, MO: Youth in Need provides services to youth on the streets. Some kids receive shelter. Other youth want to remain independent, so they receive food, clothing, or both. It is up to clients to choose what services they will receive.

Model: _____

Roles: _____

TUCSON, AZ: At the Family Counseling Center, the case managers are gatekeepers for services. Most of their clients come from a hospital discharge planner. They interview clients over the phone to determine eligibility. The services they furnish are short term.

Model: _____

Roles: _____

MITCHELL, SD: Mitchell Area Adjustment Training Center provides one-stop shopping for its clients. It has a residential program, a day program, and an independent living program. Clients enter needing residential care; the goal for most is independent living.

Model: _____

Roles: _____

·············● Exercise 2: Role Ratings

1. Rate yourself on your ability at this moment to assume each of the following eight roles:

Role	Ready and able!	Not sure	No way!
Advocate			
Broker			
Coordinator			
Consultant			
Counselor			
Planner			
Problem solver			
Record keeper			

2. What roles present the greatest challenges for you?

_____

_____

_____

_____

3. How can you improve your knowledge and skills in these areas?

_____

_____

_____

_____

·············● Exercise 3: Models and You

You have your choice of the three Case Management models in which to work. Make your choice and describe the skills and strengths you have that will help you be an effective case manager in this model.

_____

_____

_____

●●●●●●●●●●●● Exercise 4: Models and Jobs

Read the two job announcements that follow. They are reprinted here from Chapter 3 in *Generalist Case Management*.

Job Announcement 1: Case Manager

<u>Summary:</u>
The Innovative Drug Team is part of the local government's program to serve those in the criminal justice system who have a dual diagnosis of substance abuse and mental health issues. The case manager will work with a team to prepare treatment plans with multiple-problem clients who are facing adjudication.

<u>Duties and Responsibilities:</u>
Provide case management and substance abuse/mental health counseling to clients in the Innovative Drug Team

Work with team to create treatment plans

Monitor and document implementation

Write reports

Conduct assessments and present recommendations to the court

Provide counseling to in-patient clients

Perform drug testing

Be involved in professional development

<u>Minimum Job Requirements:</u>
Work experience with diverse client populations. At least two years working in community-based setting. At least one year in residential or inpatient treatment. Be familiar with case management; be familiar with substance abuse; be familiar with mental health issues. Bachelor's degree in psychology, social work, human services, public health, or related field; or Certification as a Drug and Alcohol Counselor.

Job Announcement 2: Case Manager/Administrator

<u>Summary:</u>
Oversees and administers all aspects of a specialized, community-focused case management program designed to serve the needs of a selected target population, to include supervision, training, and support of the operational and administrative duties of case managers. Provides case management services to individuals referred from domestic violence shelters. Compiles and prepares educational materials as necessary.

<u>Duties and Responsibilities:</u>

Supervises and trains case managers and associated support staff

Administers the day-to-day activities of the program

Oversees quality of case management program

Carries a caseload of clients as a case manager

Reviews case management records to evaluate quality

Maintains confidentiality of records

Develops educational materials

Supervises staff

Performs miscellaneous job-related duties as assigned

<u>Minimum Job Requirements:</u>

Bachelor's degree in human services, social work, psychology, nursing, or directly related behavioral health field; at least three years of experience that is directly related to the duties and responsibilities specified.

<u>Knowledge, Skills, and Abilities Required:</u>

Has administrative skills

Has communication skills

Understands and implements confidentiality policies

Supervises case managers for organizational and time management skills

Knows how to use community resources

Has case management knowledge, skills, and abilities

Is able to gather data, assess information, and write reports

Can supervise staff

Can write reports and other written documents

Fosters cooperation

1. You are going to apply for one of these positions. Which one and why?

_____

_____

_____

_____

2. Which of the three models is applicable to the position you chose?

_____

_____

3. List the three case management roles that you believe are critical in this position.

_____

_____

_____

4. Is the position a match with your knowledge and skills? Explain.

_____

_____

_____

_____

Exercise 5: Your Ideal Job

Write an advertisement for your ideal job. Think about your preferences and strengths in terms of clientele, knowledge, skills, and experiences. Clearly articulate the case management model and the required roles and responsibilities.

_____

_____

_____

_____

_____

_____

_____

_____

_____

_____

In More Depth: The "PACT" Model

PACT or ACT, acronyms that are often used interchangeably, illustrates the "whys and hows" of service model development. Started in 1972, this model has sustained itself over time and has grown to have a national scope. The model is perhaps best known as PACT (Program of Assertive Community Treatment) or ACT (Assertive Community Treatment); variations of its name include Community Support Programs (Wisconsin), Florida Assertive Community Treatment, and Mobile Treatment Teams (Delaware and Rhode Island). Other programs claim to be programs of assertive community treatment but meet neither the definition of PACT model nor the PACT Model Standards. This section examines the development of the PACT model and how it operates today. As you read about this model of service delivery and its development, think about how the three models discussed in Chapter 3 are applied in PACT's method of service delivery.

During the late 1960s and early 1970s, mental hospitals were being depopulated, a national trend known as deinstitutionalization. People with severe mental illnesses were discharged from institutional settings to communities with inadequate services and supports. As a result, a phenomenon referred to as "the revolving door" occurred. Many people were living substandard lives that often included homelessness, substance abuse, and jail and ended up cycling through hospitals periodically. Some help was available for those in crisis, but in reality, no comprehensive case management existed. Community mental health centers were not as effective for people with severe mental illnesses, and although they were established to serve the people discharged from hospitals, the centers actually served healthier people. These factors led professionals at Mendota Mental Health Hospital in Madison (one of two Wisconsin state hospitals) to attempt to treat more effectively the people who were trapped in the revolving door syndrome.

Economic considerations also contributed significantly to the need for a shift in services. In Los Angeles, for example, a study of high users of in-patient psychiatric services tracked the admissions and discharges of all Medi-Cal patients. This tracking allowed the county to determine the cost and the number of patients who were using psychiatric in-patient services. The study found that in six months the approximately 1,000 admissions had an average stay of six days. Most importantly, a small number of patients were hospitalized at a much higher rate than all others in that time. Those 66 patients had 480 admissions for a total of 3,330+ days hospitalized. Considering these figures by individual patient, each had an average of 7.2 admissions and 50.5 days of hospitalization during six months, costing a total of approximately $22,000. Another way to consider these statistics is to annualize them. Examining them on a yearly basis, each patient would spend 101 days out of 365 hospitalized at a cost of $44,000 per year. In its proposal for an intensive case management program for the highest users who are the most severely and persistently mentally ill, the Los Angeles County Department of Mental Health projects that reducing the hospitalization days for the 40 highest users by 30 percent would translate into savings of more than $550,000/year. So a financial incentive exists to address the needs of those who experience this "revolving door" phenomenon.

The PACT model that began in Wisconsin offers a less restrictive alternative to inpatient, often involuntary treatment, proposing instead a treatment model of effective community-based, outreach-oriented service for people with severe and persistent mental illness. Specifically, the model mandates treatment, rehabilitation, and support services to help consumers spend more time in independent living situations and more time employed in the community. Information about services and staff will help you to understand this model of service delivery more fully.

PACT aims to provide a complete care package that includes treatment within the community (rather than institutional offices), a high level of staff support, a high staff-to-client ratio, an emphasis on practical activities of daily living, and a team approach to case management. Specifically, this approach helps people live in regular housing, socialize in the community, and return to school or work. Addressing basic needs such as housing, medical care, and income enables consumers to regain stability, spend much less time in hospitals, and begin recovery. This intense case management meets PACT Standards that include service delivery where consumers live, work, and spend their leisure time; daily staff meetings; an overall 1:10 staff-to-consumer ratio; for each 50 consumers a minimum of 16 hours/week of psychiatrist time must be provided to the agency.

The challenges of PACT are best illustrated by the consumers it serves. Three case descriptions illustrate who the severely mentally ill are and the problems they have.

Case 1

Shelly has a borderline personality disorder. After working with her a couple of years, the team believes that she has more than one diagnosis, including mental retardation. Records have been requested but not yet received. At age 33, she has been a high user of emergency room services for seven or eight years. The psychiatrist knows her from his days as a resident. At that time, she would come in every couple of weeks. They would keep her in the emergency room overnight and then discharge her the next day. She remained stable with this level of services. With the change in the legal system—doctors being sued for failure to provide adequate care—the emergency room staff don't like to discharge anyone from the emergency room. Their preference is to transfer the individual to an inpatient facility and pass responsibility to another physician. Now Shelly goes to the emergency room and is then hospitalized. Patient costs for Shelly exceeded $150,000 last year.

Shelly presents a number of challenges. She's very impulsive and hard to work with. She doesn't remember things; you can tell her something and 10 minutes later she's forgotten it. She is also abusive with her language and physically violent. Although she's never harmed anyone, she has smashed windows and broken furniture. This makes it difficult to place her in board-and-care facilities. At three different facilities, she has accused the staff of raping or molesting her. These charges require investigation. And although never proven, these investigations are unpleasant, and it is time consuming to file a report, process it, and investigate. So for many reasons, board-and-care facilities don't want her.

Another problem is that Shelly uses crack. She receives a sizable check, larger than most. Because her father died before she was an adult, she draws his Social Security as well as her own Social Security income. She uses this money to buy drugs. The plan was to move her to a locked facility, get her off crack, stabilize her medication, and show her there is a benefit to all this. Eventually she would move to a less restrictive environment. It is a great plan; unfortunately neither the Institute of Mental Disease nor any locked facilities will take her. The state hospital is not an option because it is downsizing. There are almost 700 state hospital beds in the state. Eighty percent of them belong to this county because it has the largest population of mentally ill people. So Shelly presents a number of challenges.

Case 2

Sue came to case management services in an interesting way. The staff was evaluating another potential client at the hospital when the case manager recognized Sue from a previous job and asked, "What are you doing here?" At this time, Sue was very psychotic. She is a 43-year-old African American who had come to the hospital because she had been off her medications for several months. She had been living in an unlicensed board-and-care facility and was raped by her male roommate. No attempts had been made to have her seen by a psychiatrist to get medication. She was floridly psychotic, yet out of all that psychosis, she recognized the case manager and told her what had been happening. The case manager offered case management services, and she accepted. She became more stabilized in the hospital but still needed some ongoing treatment. The case manager visited her at the board-and-care facility, called licensing immediately, and had them cited. Sue moved out of that facility to a licensed facility that had a contract with the Department of Mental Health. Being in a licensed facility means that clients are offered more services, provided psychiatric appointments, and transported to medical appointments.

Sue made good progress and, along the way, began to remember things that had happened to her in the past few years. In one psychotic episode, she had painted her kitchen cabinets in her apartment with red nail polish and done other damage, which got her evicted. She also had three children. Her 17-year-old daughter had just emancipated herself, having had enough of the craziness. Her 16-year-old son and 5-year-old daughter went to live with her brother because by then she was homeless and didn't want them on the streets with her. During the next few years, her brother, unbeknownst to her, sought guardianship of her children. As she became more stable, she realized that she was going to lose custody of her children. This proved to be a powerful motivator. She contacted Children's Services to find out what she needed to do to regain her children. Sue was told, "You have to have a job and an apartment that is a suitable living environment for a child. You have to be on medication and involved in counseling on a regular basis."

With the help of her case manager, she did it all—but in small steps. The case manager suggested, "Let's take it one step at a time. Have you thought about getting a job? What would you like to do? Maybe sheltered workshop where you could work in a structured environment?" She got a job as a substitute cafeteria helper, working three hours a day from 10 a.m. to 1 p.m. She gets a bit of money from that to supplement her SSI. She did all that on her own. Sue also found out that some subsidized apartments were going to become available. She got an application and, with the case manager's help, completed it. She went for an interview and rented an apartment. These apartments also have a case manager on staff who is there to assist the residents. Sue returned to Children's Services and was told that she would need to petition the court. The case manager contacted an attorney and petitioned the courts. She survived home visits from social workers, and she got custody of her daughter.

So this is one of the successful stories although Sue is now finding out it is very difficult living with a 10-year old. She still works, and she is still on her medications, although one was an older anti-psychotic that has some side effects. Her case manager encouraged her to switch to a new medication, and she is doing fine. She takes one pill at night rather than several throughout the day; it helps her sleep, and she wakes up with energy and enthusiasm. Her vision has also improved. Her case manager still follows her, just visiting to see if she's doing okay.

Case 3

Robert is living on the streets. He doesn't want to go to a board-and-care home. He wants his own place but can't budget his money well enough to live independently. He won't accept anything less. It is hard to see him living on the streets because he is living like an animal. His money lasts through the first two weeks of the month and then he is broke. He is panhandling and sleeping on street corners. The agency put him on a payee status with his Social Security so that he can't blow the money the way he has been. This means he has to bring this guardian to receive his checks. Robert is angry right now; he sees this requirement as punishment.

Conclusion

These three cases illustrate the complexities of work with this particular client group. Much of PACT's effectiveness comes from a "one-stop-shopping" approach. Direct, integrated services bring medical and psychiatric treatment, rehabilitation services, and community support services to severely mentally ill consumers who would probably receive few or no services unless they were in a crisis.

This approach is successful for a number of reasons. Staff are available 24 hours a day, 7 days a week. The majority of services are delivered where a consumer lives and works. Consumers work with a case management team. Teams consist of psychiatrists, nurses, social workers, mental health professionals, substance abuse treatment specialists, vocational rehabilitation counselors, and case managers. Consumers are often team members themselves as providers and peer counselors. Another strength of PACT is its early and continuous involvement of a consumer's family members as support for the consumer, members of a PACT advisory group, and in some cases, as a consumer's case manager. Finally, consumers are encouraged to try new things, actively participate as collaborators with their team, and when able, function as their own case manager. This comprehensive approach has proven to be more effective than the usual office-based mental health system (Edgar, 2001, 2002; McFarlane et al., 2000; Kenny, Calsyn, & Morse, 2004).

Exercise 6: "It's a good PACT day!"

Candace and Donovan work in a PACT program; Candace is a team leader and social worker and Donovan is a case manager. Go to the website that accompanies this book: www.thomsonedu.com/counseling/mcclam, Chapter 3, Link 1, to listen as they talk about their program and their work. Then answer the following questions.

1. How does Candace's description of the PACT program where she works illustrate the PACT model you read about?

   Program focus:

   _____

   _____

   _____

   Staff:

   _____

   _____

   _____

   Clients:

   _____

   _____

   _____

   _____

2. How does the PACT staff handle medications?

   _____

   _____

   _____

   _____

3. Describe a typical day for Donovan.

   _____

   _____

   _____

   _____

4. Describe the roles that Candace and Donovan perform in their work.

_____

_____

_____

_____

5. What is "a good PACT day"?

_____

_____

_____

_____

Self-Assessment

The following activity will help you assess what you have learned from Chapter 3. Think about what you now know and the additional information that would help you expand your knowledge about the models of case management.

1. Suppose you worked for a PACT program. Consider the cases in the PACT model and the words of Candace and Donovan. What would be most challenging for you if you were a case manager?

_____

_____

_____

_____

2. What roles would be easiest for you?

_____

_____

_____

Most difficult?

_____

_____

_____

3. What skills do you have that would make you an effective case manager in the PACT model?

_____

_____

_____

4. What questions do you have about models, roles, and/or PACT?

_____

_____

_____

 # Pretest Answers

1. Eighteen-year-old substance abuser: broker to link with needed services, coordinator to integrate services, or planner to prepare client for services and treatment.

   Forty-five year-old parolee: problem solver to help client become self-sufficient, counselor to maintain relationship with client and family, or advocate to speak on behalf of client.

   Pregnant teen: planner to determine actions; problem solver to figure out what to do; counselor to deal with difficult issues and choices.

   Middle-school student: consultant to teacher; coordinator of services; planner about actions and services.

   Twin sisters: counselor to help deal with end-of-life issues; problem solver to explore resolutions to any problems; broker to match clients with services.

   Daughter of elderly mother: problem solver to figure out how to get more intensive care; broker to match client with services; advocate to speak for client.

2. Goals: Role based (meet needs through single point of access, act to link/provide/monitor services, roles vary according to the function and services provided, p. 61); organization based (meet multiple needs through single point of access with one location for delivery, act to coordinate services or lead a team of professionals, nature of case management determined by organizational structure and how services are delivered, p. 65); responsibility based (transition of care from professionals to nonprofessionals, act to support and train nonprofessionals to provide continuing case management, emphasis on short- and long-term involvement of case management, coordination of services, help of volunteers, and empowerment of clients, p. 67).

3. Model for my grandfather: Organization, services in one location to meet multiple needs.

References

Allnes, D., & Knoedler, W. (2003, June). National Program Standards for ACT Teams. Retrieved April 18, 2006, from http://www.nami.org/Content/ContentGroups/Programs/PACT1/NationalStandardsfor ACTeams.pdf.

Edgar, E. (2001, Fall). Assertive community treatment provides jail diversion. *NAMI Advocate*, 28.

Edgar, E. (2002, Winter). Did you know that assertive community treatment helps consumers with housing? *NAMI Advocate*, 28.

Kenny, D. A., Calsyn, R. J., & Morse, G. A. (2004). Evaluation of treatment programs for persons with severe mental illness: Moderator and mediator effects. *Evaluation Review*, 28(4), 294–324.

McFarlane, W. R., Dushay, R. A., Deakins, S. M., Stastny, P., Lukens, E. P., Toran, J., et al. (2000). Employment outcomes in family-aided assertive community treatment. *American Journal of Orthopsychiatry*, 70(2), 203–214.

The Assessment Phase of Case Management

The concept and practice of assessment, the first phase of case management, is introduced in Chapter 4 of *Generalist Case Management*. Case management in this phase involves application for services, case assignment, and documentation and report writing. The following exercises provide opportunities for you to practice your skills in these areas.

 Pretest

When you finish reading Chapter 4 in *Generalist Case Management*, answer the following questions and complete the items.

1. Distinguish between structured and unstructured interviews.

_____

_____

_____

_____

2. What are the responsibilities of the interviewer or case manager at the initial contact?

_____

_____

_____

3. When and how does an applicant become a client or customer of an agency or organization?

_____

_____

_____

4. Describe the three ways case assignment may occur.

_____

_____

_____

Chapter Summary

The process of case management usually begins when an individual in need seeks help from another source. Often, the individual will use informal resources first, such as friends, family, parents, or children. When someone decides that help is advantageous, he or she may get in touch with a human service agency. Case management may also begin if an individual is already involved with another human service agency, and he or she has needs that go beyond the provisions of that agency. In this case, the person is referred to a new agency. After the initial contact with an applicant for services, the case manager begins the assessment phase of case management. During this phase, the case manager gathers information from the client and determines eligibility for services. This phase includes the initial contact, the intake interview, a discussion of confidentiality and privileged communication, and the evaluation of available information to determine eligibility.

Throughout the assessment phase of case management, documentation and report writing are critical. Different agencies may require different forms of documentation, but typically during the assessment phase, it includes intake summaries and staff notes. Intake summaries usually include information about the applicant, the presenting problem, a summary of his or her background and social history, the case manager's diagnostic impressions, and treatment recommendations. Staff notes, or case notes, are also important documentation during assessment. These notes are written after each interaction between the applicant and the professional and are filed chronologically in the client's chart. The format for staff notes varies depending on the agency guidelines.

Exercise 1: The Initial Interview—The Applicant's Perspective

Those served by case managers have a lot to teach us about case management and helping. The following accounts relate the experiences of three applicants as they describe their initial interview with a case manager.

1. Read the following three applicant accounts of the initial meeting with a caseworker.

Client I

I made a (self-referral) telephone appointment to talk with a caseworker who briefly advised me to bring documentation of current earnings, my most recent tax return, a current rent receipt and telephone bill, a copy of my separation or divorce decree, and a current bank statement (and other records, ad infinitum) with me to our meeting. The site of our meeting was a day-care center located near several housing projects and homes. This center helps families find in-home child care for residents from all parts of the city. When I arrived for my early morning appointment, the receptionist asked me to take a seat. After waiting one half hour beyond my scheduled appointment time, the receptionist called my name and escorted me to the office of the front-line worker who would interview me.

The caseworker was sitting behind her desk talking on the phone and motioned for me to take a seat. I again waited at length while she completed her telephone conversation. At that point, she acknowledged me with a rather perfunctory, "Sorry to keep you waiting. It's been a crazy morning. Have any problem finding us? Good. Let's get started. Did you bring all the documentation that we'll need? Let's see what we have here."—all in one breath. The desk that separated us served as a physical barrier to any feelings of warmth, caring, interest, acceptance, or respect that I would have welcomed. In fact, I remember feeling that she was contemptuous of me; but I wonder, in retrospect, whether my own distaste at having to ask for assistance or respect influenced my perceptions. The caseworker immediately delved into evaluating and processing reams of application paperwork. She was not interested in any other aspect of my life. She never asked if I needed any other help, financial or otherwise. She didn't offer information on any other resources that might have been available to me. In fact, she rarely made eye contact, but remained detached and businesslike. The experience felt much more like an interrogation than an interview. She fired questions at me, as she demanded each document that I was required to bring with me. "How much money do you receive from the child's father each week? Why don't you want to place your child in our day-care program instead of the satellite program? If it's that inconvenient for you to get here, how did you get here today? You indicated that you don't own a car—how did you get here today? Whose car is it?"

At the conclusion of our meeting, she explained the accounting procedures, indicating that I would pay the agency directly for services rendered by a satellite caregiver. Payment would be based on sliding scale based upon my income and ability to pay. She then dismissed me, never getting up from her desk, as she advised me that I would hear from her just as soon as my application was reviewed for acceptance by her supervisor. In fact, I did not hear from her at all but received a phone call from the day-care center.

2. List what you learned NOT to do in the initial interview.

_____

_____

_____

_____

_____

_____

3. Rewrite each negative you listed in question 2 as a positive statement that will guide your behavior as a helping professional in the initial interview.

_____

_____

_____

_____

_____

Client II

I don't think anyone ever told me exactly what their job was. See I was very subservient to anybody in that area because I was scared to death. I mean literally scared. I had a phobia of failing and having everything jerked out from under me.

Here's what I think a caseworker should do. Clients are not numbers so they shouldn't be treated like Client Number 4622 or a Social Security number. When you tell a client that the appointment is at 3:00 p.m., then the appointment is at 3:00 p.m. Nothing should interfere with that. I am going to treat my clients that way.

I think clients are already intimidated before they ever come in. They have a feeling that the help could be taken away at any time. That is something else every caseworker should do, reassure the client that as long as they fulfill their obligations, they can't lose the help they are getting. That was one of my biggest fears, and I was so afraid of it, I would not even ask. I would not even bring the subject up.

4. List what you learned NOT to do in the initial interview.

_____

_____

_____

_____

_____

5. Rewrite each negative you listed in Item 4 as a positive statement that will guide your behavior as a helping professional in the initial interview.

_____

_____

_____

_____

_____

Client III

The very first time I went to a meeting at DHS was to get help for myself, my daughter, and my ex-husband. When I went back the second time to apply for assistance for myself and my daughter, I ended up getting a really wonderful worker. I was walking on eggshells and I didn't know where to go. I didn't know what to do. I had no self-esteem, no self-respect. I was in the gutter, literally, and I didn't know where to go. And didn't know which end was up. My worker helped me.

I had another worker though who was awful. I had already started school and my worker changed. I went to this other worker, and she made me feel like dirt: "Here you are getting benefits, and you are not doing anything to help yourself. You are not even trying to find a job." It was just like I was a nobody. She didn't give me anything, and here I was doing everything I could. I was on welfare, and I was a welfare mother, and that was all I was ever likely to be. In fact, I did go to her supervisor over that because it did hurt. And by that point I was strong enough to really voice how I felt. Had I had her in the beginning, I don't think I would have been able to do anything about it, but later on when I gained the confidence through going back to school and through support group meetings, and counseling, I was able to see that what she was doing wasn't fair to me. In fact, she ended up being taken off case management in DHS.

6. List what you learned NOT to do in the initial interview.

_____

_____

_____

_____

_____

7. Rewrite each negative you listed in Item 6 as a positive statement that will guide your behavior as a helping professional in the initial interview.

_____

_____

_____

_____

_____

·············● Exercise 2: The Initial Interview Summary

One purpose of the intake interview is to assess an individual's eligibility for services. The intake interview form in this exercise has information that was gathered during an interview at a mental health facility. A case manager interviewed a person who was referred by professionals at the hospital. Eligibility for services is determined by matching needs with services. The treatment team that will review the intake information includes a social worker, the intake case manager, a nurse, a physician, and the director of psychiatric services to determine eligibility. Before the treatment team meets, each member will read an intake summary prepared by the case manager.

You are charged with preparing the intake interview summary. At this facility the summary is organized around the following items:

✦ Worker's name, date of contact, date of summary
✦ Applicant's demographic data: for example, name, address, phone number, agency applicant, Social Security number
✦ Source of information during the intake interview
✦ Presenting problem
✦ Summary of background and social history related to the problem
✦ Previous contact with agency
✦ Diagnosis summary statement
✦ Treatment recommendations

1. Read the intake interview form carefully. If some of the abbreviations are unfamiliar to you, see the legend at the end of the form.

☐ *Hospital*
☐ *Outpatient*
☐ *Outreach Program*
☐ *In-Home Program*

Pt. Chart # 44179
Date: X/XX/XX   *Time: 2240*

SCREENING and SOCIAL ASSESSMENT FORM

NAME: _____ Age <u>12</u> Male ☐   Female ☒

REFERRAL SOURCE: <u>Metropolitan Hospital</u>   Informant (relationship): <u>parents</u>

ADDRESS:

_____

PRESENTING PROBLEMS: <u>Ct wrote suicide note and gave to friend at school. Mother reports ct was sexually molested by stepfather and has to go to court on Wednesday to testify. Mother reports ct is increasingly frightened and depressed. Reportedly stepfather told ct that if she told about molestation he would hurt her and kidnap her so she couldn't see her mother again. Wed. will be first day that ct has seen stepfather in almost a year. Mother reports that ct reported that abuse lasted for approx. 2yrs. 9 months. Ct has threatened suicide in past but never attempted.</u>

CURRENT LIVING/FAMILY SITUATION: <u>lives with mother. M reports neighborhood safe; no siblings.</u>

_____

How have your current problems affected family, job, or school? <u>Mother reports that ct's grades have suffered and that mother has had to miss a lot of work. Reports ↑ stress.</u>

Lives at Home Alone: ☐ Yes ☒ No Describe: <u>N/A</u>

_____

_____

Lives at Home with Family: ☒ Yes ☐ No Describe: <u>lives with mother</u>

_____

EDUCATION:

Educational/Vocational History: Highest Grade Completed: <u>6th</u>   Where?: <u>South Elem.</u>

Employed? ☒ No ☐ Yes (How long? <u>N/A</u>   ) (Where? <u>N/A</u>   )

Military Service? ☒ No ☐ Yes Branch: <u>N/A</u>   When? <u>N/A</u>   Type of Discharge: <u>N/A</u>

LEGAL:
Have there been any legal problems? Give dates—current or resolved: <u>denies</u>

_____

_____

Family History of Violent Crimes? ☒ No ☐ Yes   If Yes, Describe:

<u>denies</u>

_____

_____

History of DUI? ☒ No   ☐ Yes   Dates:

<u>denies</u> _____

SUICIDE/HOMICIDE HISTORY: (Includes past/present attempts, ideation, plan.) List dates and specific behaviors and quotes by potential patient and significant others:

Current: <u>wrote suicide note and gave to peer</u> _____

Past: <u>has threatened in past but never attempted</u> _____

Family History for Suicide/Homicide: <u>a cousin at age 13, and great great grandfather</u> _____

Prior Psychiatric Treatment: ☐ *Inpatient*   ☒ *Outpatient*   ☐ *None*
Prior Alcohol/Drug Treatment: ☐ *Inpatient*   ☐ *Outpatient*   ☒ *None*

<u>IN-PT. TREATMENT</u>	<u>THERAPIST/M.D.</u>	<u>DATE</u>
_____	_____	_____
_____	_____	_____

<u>OUT-PT. TREATMENT</u>	<u>THERAPIST</u>	<u>DATE</u>
<u>private</u>	<u>Jacinta Lopez</u>	<u>since June</u>
_____	_____	_____

SLEEP:

Sleep Disturbance (nightmares, sleepwalking, enuresis, etc.) ☐ *No* ☒ *Yes,* *Describe:* <u>M reports ct talks in</u> <u>sleep and that she experiences nightmares about SF</u> _____

_____

Sleep Pattern: Amount (hrs./night) <u>8</u> *Recent change:* ☒ *No* ☐ *Yes Insomnia?*   ☒ *No*   ☐ *Yes*
Describe: <u>N/A</u> _____

_____

Hypersomnia? ☒ *No*   ☐ *Yes Sleep routine (meds, toys, nightlight, etc.)* <u>shower and brush teeth; sleeps c radio on</u>

_____

APPETITE: *Any appetite problems?* ☐ *No* ☒ *Yes If yes, please explain:* <u>M reports doesn't eat in a.m.</u> *Weight Loss?*
☒ *No* ☐ *Yes   How much?* <u>N/A</u>

ALCOHOL/DRUG HISTORY: List drugs/alcohol used past/present: ☒ None

Alcohol/Drug	Amount/Frequency	Dates of Last Use	How Long Used
denies			

History of Blackouts? ☒ No   ☐ Yes   *Explain:*

N/A _____

Use/Share Needles? ☒ No   ☐ Yes   *Explain:*

N/A _____

How does Client feel drug/alcohol use is interfering with life and/or affecting health?

N/A _____

_____

_____

Has Client tried to quit on own? ☒ No   ☐ Yes   *Explain:*

N/A _____

_____

Did Client have any withdrawal symptoms when trying to quit? ☒ No   ☐ Yes   *Explain:*

N/A _____

_____

_____

Do any family members/significant others have a problem with drugs and/or alcohol?
☒ No   ☐ Yes   *Explain:*
denies _____

ACTIVITIES OF DAILY LIVING:
Bathing, Dressing, without assistance? ☒ Yes   ☐ No
Cooks, Sleeps, Feeds Self without assistance? ☒ Yes   ☐ No
Drives, Uses Transportation without assistance? ☒ Yes   ☐ No
Reads, Writes without assistance? ☒ Yes   ☐ No
Uses, Manages Money without assistance? ☒ Yes   ☐ No
Takes Prescribed Medications without assistance? ☒ Yes   ☐ No

PAST/PRESENT MEDICAL HISTORY:
How does client describe his/her health status? Good __✓__ Fair _____ Poor _____
Family Physician: _Dr. Jones_

Illnesses:	None _____	Date	Surgery:	None _____	Date
			repair of cleft lip		_XXXX_

Was client hospitalized in the last 6 months? ☐ No ☒ Yes
For: <u>ct was held by SF illegally, when SF dropped her off, ct was hysterical, had to be taken to ER via ambulance</u>

When was the last time client saw a doctor? <u>1-2 months ago</u> *For:* <u>stomach virus</u>

DEVELOPMENTAL HISTORY:

Did client's Mother have any problems during pregnancy, labor, delivery? ☒ No ☐ Yes
Explain: <u>None other than having cleft lip</u>

Did client meet developmental milestones within normal limits? ☐ No ☒ Yes
Explain: <u>Everything was normal</u>

RELIGIOUS/CULTURAL HISTORY: <u>Baptist. M reports that will not interfere c TX</u>

HISTORY OF SELF-INFLICTED WOUNDS (CARVINGS)? ☒ No ☐ Yes

HISTORY OF PHYSICAL/SEXUAL ABUSE/MOLESTATION/RAPE: ☐ No ☒ Yes
Explain: <u>sexually abused by SF for approx. 2 yrs. 9 mon.</u>

OBSERVATION CHECKLIST *(Adolescents/Adults)*

	DISORDERD CONDUCT		AFFECTIVE DISORDERS		ATTENTION DISORDERS
	Curfew Violations	X	Depressed or Irritable Mood		Easily Distracted
	Often Lies		Apathy or Indifference		Reckless, Takes Chances
	Vandalism		Weight Loss or Gain		Often Not Listening
	Thefts (include Family)		Appetite Changes		Can't Finish a Task
	Car Thefts/Joyriding		Insomnia/Hypersomnia		Seems "Wired/Hyper"
X	Fights Adults		Fatigue/Loss of Energy		Restless
	Satanic Cult	X	Feelings of Worthlessness	X	Trouble with Decision Making
	Used Weapon in Fight		Hyperactive		Can't Concentrate
	Temper Fits in Which Property Is Destroyed		Pressured Speech		Has Been on Ritalin
	School Refusal		Giddy/Inappropriate Laughter		Psychotic Disorders
	Runs Away Overnight		Grandiosity		Confused/Confusing
	Truancy		Bursts of Aggression		Odd Use of Words
	Shoplifting		Racing Thoughts		Isolation/Withdrawal
	Selling Drugs		Poor Concentration		Feels Like in a Dream
	Fights Peers				Hallucinations
	Committed Sexual Assault		Rapid Mood Swings		Bizarre Behavior
	School Suspension		Crying Spells		Presence of Absent People
	Physical Cruelty to People	X	Recent Suicide Ideation		Odd Beliefs
	Disregard of Parental Limits		Recent Suicide Plan		Intense Jealousy
	Fire Setting		Recent Suicide Attempt		Fears Others out to Get Them
	Cruelty to Animals		Incontinent/Enuresis		

MENTAL STATUS: *(Circle applicable information)*

Appearance: drab; unkempt; atypical clothing; (well-groomed;) meticulous; obese; underweight; younger than stated age; older than stated age.
Describe: _____

_____

_____

Attitude/Mood: sad; euphoric; labile; hostile; irritable; (apathetic;) resistive; cooperative; sarcastic; defensive; resentful; (detached;) suspicious; uncooperative; overly compliant; hysterical; fearful; angry.
Describe: _____

_____

_____

Affect: (flat;) blunted; tearful; appropriate to mood; inappropriate to mood; bright; disdainful; nonchalant; hostile.
Describe: _____

_____

_____

Nonverbal Behavior: holds one position for prolonged period; (slumps while sitting;) good posture; rigid, stiff movements; (obviously tense;) jerking; spastic movements; frequent, startled responses; trance-like; nervous, repetitive movements; posturing; agitated; impulsive; avoids eye contact; psychomotor retardation; restless; (hyperactive;) seductive; anxious; threatening; physically aggressive; shakiness; paranoia.
Describe: _____

_____

_____

Speech: (seems appropriate;) overtalkative; talkative; slowed; pressured; slurred; mute; stutter; monotone; soft; irrelevant; verbally aggressive; dramatic; rambling; obscene language; unintelligible; rapid; talks to self.
Describe: _____

_____

_____

Thought Process: grandiose; (self depreciative;) flight of ideas; loose associations; ideas of reference; delusions; hallucinations; phobias; tangential paranoia; confused; peculiar body sensations.
Describe: _____

_____

_____

Memory: recent impaired; (recent intact;) remote impaired; remote intact; poor concentration.
Describe: _____

_____

Orientation: (alert;) (oriented;) disoriented to time; disoriented to place; disoriented to person; disoriented to circumstances.
Describe: _____

_____

ACTIVE PLANS/RECOMMENDATION/FORMULATION
Inpt. _____

_____

_____

Recommendation:　　☒ *Inpatient*　　☐ *Outpatient*　　☐ *Other*

Physician Assigned:　　☐ *No*　　☒ *Yes*　　*Physician Name* _____

Plan Recommendation Reviewed with Client/Patient?　　☐ *No*　　　☒ *Yes*

Vital Signs (if indicated): Temp 98°　　　P 106　　　R 20　　B/P 117/66

E. F. Fowler
_____　　　　　　_____
Admitting Licensed Nursing Staff (if applicable)　　　　　　*Referral Service Screening Staff*

PROBLEM LIST:

1.　suicidal _____

_____

2.　sexually molested _____

_____

3.　_____

_____

_____

4.　_____

_____

_____

TREATMENT PLAN:

1.　grouptx _____

_____

2.　familytx _____

_____

3.　individual contact with psychiatrist; medication management _____

4.　structure of milieu _____

5.　D/C planning _____

DISCHARGE PLAN:

1.　stabilize and refer to a less restrictive level of care _____

2.　_____

_____

_____

3.

_____

_____

4.

_____

_____

5.

_____

_____

_____

Ted Clinton   Clinical Assistant

_____

*Alonzo Hernandes   Clinical Team Leader/Clinical Director

*The above signature indicates that the Clinical Team Leader/Director has reviewed this data for clinical completeness and will coordinate implementation of the above plans.

Legend: Abbreviations used in form:

ct	client
sf	stepfather
N/A	not applicable
c	with
tx	treatment
dc	discharge

2. Using the blank form, write an intake summary using the headings listed to organize your report. The information you include in the intake summary comes directly from the screening and social assessment form YOU JUST READ.

INTAKE SUMMARY

Pt. Chart No. _____   Name _____

Interviewer _____   Date_____

_____

_____

_____

_____

_____

_____

_____   _____
Case Manager's Signature   Date

---

3. What difficulties did you encounter "putting the pieces of the puzzle" together?

_____

_____

_____

4. Did you need more information to write the summary? What additional information would you like to have?

_____

_____

_____

5. Are you confident of your recommendations? What is the basis for your confidence or lack of confidence?

_____

_____

_____

⬤ Exercise 3: Careful Assessment

The following case studies are about Susanna, James, Samantha, and Alicia and Montford, all homeless children attending school. The principal of the school has asked you to conduct an assessment of these children and provide initial recommendations. Before you begin this exercise, go to the website that accompanies this book: www.thomsonedu.com/counseling/mcclam, Chapter 4, Link 1, to read more about homeless families and children.

1. Read the three cases that describe the situations in which Susanna, James, and Alicia find themselves.

Susanna

Susanna is 15 years old. The city where she lives has four schools, two elementary, one middle, and one high school. There are about 1,500 students enrolled in the city/county school district and about 450 in the local high school that Susanna is attending. For the past six months, Susanna has been living with her boyfriend and his parents. She is pregnant and her boyfriend's parents want her to move out of their home. Her father lives in a town with his girlfriend, about 50 miles from the city. Her mother lives outside the city with Susanna's baby brother. Right now Susanna's mother is receiving child support for the two children. Susanna wants to have a portion of the child support so that she can find a place of her own to live. Her mother says that the only way that Susanna can have access to that money is to move back home. Susanna refuses to move back in with her mother.

You receive a call from the school counselor at Susanna's high school. Susanna's mother is at the school, demanding that Susanna be withdrawn from school. Susanna's mother indicates that Susanna will be moving in with her and will be enrolling in another school district.

Currently Susanna is not doing very well in school. She misses school and she tells the counselor it is because she is tired and that she does not have good food to eat. She has not told the counselor that she is looking for a place to live. Right now she is failing two of her classes and she has 1 B and 2 Ds. Her boyfriend has missed a lot of school, too.

James and Samantha

James is 10 years old and he has a sister, Samantha, who is 8. At the beginning of the school year, both of the children were attending Boone Elementary School. Both children live with their aunt and uncle; their parents are in prison. In the middle of the school year, the aunt picked up the children one afternoon and told them that they were going to move that evening. They picked up their clothes and a few toys and moved into a shelter. They didn't know that this was a shelter for women and children who were being abused. The children were brokenhearted to leave their school. They had good friends there; James was head of the safety patrol and was the star of the choir and drama club. Samantha played with her best friend Carrie every day and all of her friends called her the "teacher's pet." Samantha says that she understands why she needs to go to another school, but James is angry that he has to transfer. Finally, the staff at the shelter tried to work out transportation back to the school. School officials told James's and Samantha's aunt that the children could not transfer back into the old district. The school counselor has referred James and Samantha to you.

Alicia and Montford

About a year ago, Alicia and Montford moved into the New Horizon homeless shelter for families. They have been living there with mom and dad for the past six months. The family may only stay at the shelter until the end of the month. The assistant principal at the local elementary school just called you to ask for assistance. Both Alicia and Montford are not performing very well in school and they are constantly fighting with their classmates and with their teachers. Neither of the children can read at grade level. Both have low math scores, and they have limited social skills. For example, yesterday Montford hit a kindergarten girl because she broke in line in front of him. He told his teacher to "go to hell" when she took him to the principal's office. He never completes his work and never brings his homework to school. If the teacher sends a report home for his mom and dad to sign, he does not return the form.

Alicia tries to fade into the background at school. But she is equally unresponsive. She will not talk in class to her classmates or to her teacher. She just sits in the classroom and stares or puts her head on her desk. At recess she sits in the corner by herself. If she is "made" to play with the other children, she cries and runs off.

Because the state tests begin in the next month, the teacher and the principal are concerned about Alicia's and Montford's scores. The school has been on probation because of the regulations from "No Child Left Behind." Every score is important to the school administration. You have been called to talk with the parents about motivating these two children.

2. Describe your reactions to each of these students and how they find counselors. Discuss their parents and the relationship they have with them.

Susanna:

_____

_____

_____

James and Samantha:

_____

_____

_____

Alicia and Montford:

_____

_____

_____

3. Sometimes we write about our clients using subjective language instead of objective language. Making interpretations, failing to indicate the sources of our information, and labeling represent challenges to objective writing. Review the information you provided about Susanna, James, Samantha, Alicia, and Montford and use the following items to evaluate your objectivity.

Interpretation

List phrases that go beyond factual information. Rewrite in terms of evidence and not your own opinion.

Phrase 1: Beyond factual information

_____

Rewrite phrase 1

_____

_____

Phrase 2: Beyond factual information

_____

Rewrite phrase 2

_____

_____

Phrase 3: Beyond actual information

_____

Rewrite phrase 3

_____

_____

Citing Direct and Indirect Observation

Look for phrases that do not indicate the source of the information presented. Indicate if the information does not come from your own observation.

Phrase 1: No indication of source

_____

Rewrite phrase 1

_____

_____

Phrase 2: No indication of source

_____

Rewrite phrase 2

_____

_____

Using Labels

Sometimes it is easier to write about clients using labels that you believe communicate information about the client. Labels may be negative or positive. Look at your descriptions and indicate where you used labels to describe the client or the client's situation.

Phrase 1: Indicate where labels are used

_____

Rewrite phrase 1

_____

_____

Phrase 2: Indicate where labels are used

_____

Rewrite phrase 2

_____

_____

·············● Exercise 4: Documentation

Go to the Wadsworth website, Chapter 4, Link 2, and listen to Herman Twiggs talk about the importance of documentation in a case file.

Why does he think documentation is important?

_____

_____

_____

What do you think you need to be able to do to be good at documentation?

_____

_____

_____

Case Notes

Case or staff notes are a type of documentation that provide a written record of each interaction between a case manager and an applicant or client. Although the format for case notes varies from setting to setting, they are always an important part of the case file.

1. A beginning case manager who has six different clients made the following case notes. Critique each case note. What is helpful about the information? What questions does each case note raise?

   - 4-1-XX Client seemed in a hurry. We talked briefly about how she is dealing with her stress. Client says she is getting overwhelmed by all her responsibilities but is getting through them. She also mentioned her excitement about this weekend.

_____

_____

_____

_____

- 2-24-XX Worker observed client taking Strong Inventory Test. Worker was not there.

_____

_____

_____

_____

- 3-3-XX 2:25 p.m. Said she is okay.
- 3-5-XX 3:15 p.m. Said she was well and laughed.
  3-8-XX 2:00 p.m. Not home, left message.
        11:15 p.m. Phone was busy.
        11:30 p.m. Phone still busy.

_____

_____

_____

_____

_____

- 6-15-XX 3:30 p.m. Client stated that he was doing well, he had a "fun weekend," and identified no new problems at this time.

_____

_____

_____

- 4-1-XX I tried to contact client Sue Jones by phone today between 8:30 p.m. until 9:00 p.m. I called four different times but line was always busy. Everything should be going well.

_____

_____

_____

- 9-10-XX I called Janie to find out why she missed our appointment. She stated she forgot. She is working a lot.

_____

_____

_____

_____

● Exercise 5: First Impressions

The intake interview is a starting point to provide help. During a successful intake interview, the case manager establishes rapport with the client by demonstrating respect, empathy, and cultural sensitivity. The case manager who conducts the intake interview also presents a positive environment that ensures confidentiality, eliminates physical barriers, and promotes dialogue. Cultural insensitivity on the case manager's part may convey attitudes of sexism, racism, ethnocentrism, and/or ageism. These may occur when the case manager makes unwarranted assumptions about the client based upon his or her stereotypes of that population.

In the following clips on the Wadsworth website, Chapter 4, Link 3, three individuals relate situations where they have experienced cultural insensitivity or discrimination.

Phil

1. Listen as Phil describes an appointment for a hearing screening.

2. Describe the problem Phil experienced.

_____

_____

_____

_____

3. How did Phil feel about this experience?

_____

_____

_____

_____

4. How would these feelings help or hamper the helping relationship?

_____

_____

_____

_____

Nicole

1. Listen as Nicole shares a family experience buying a car.

2. Describe the problem Nicole experienced.

_____

_____

_____

_____

3. What is the goal of an automobile salesperson?

_____

_____

_____

4. How did Nicole feel about the experience?

_____

_____

_____

_____

5. How would her feelings help or hamper the process of closing the deal on a car?

_____

_____

_____

_____

Tracey

1. Listen as Tracey recounts an interview for a job.

2. Describe the problem Tracey experienced.

_____

_____

_____

_____

3. Explain the two assumptions that the interviewer made about Tracey.

_____

_____

_____

_____

4. How did she react to these assumptions?

_____

_____

_____

_____

5. How did Tracey feel about the interview and the interviewer?

_____

_____

_____

Conclusions

1. What do these experiences have in common?

_____

_____

_____

_____

_____

2. What have you learned from the experiences of Phil, Nicole, and Tracey?

_____

_____

_____

_____

_____

_____

 # In More Depth: Forming Impressions of Others

Chapter 4 explores conducting a beginning assessment of the client, documenting an intake interview, and writing case notes. Characteristics of quality assessment and well-written documentation include objectivity and clarity. At times the basic assumptions that case managers make about their clients prevent them from making objective assessments or writing balanced or factual case notes. When case managers make assumptions about their clients, they may have formed impressions of them without proof or factual information.

So how do we form this subjective impression of others? Let's look at four concepts that social psychology deems important in assessing others: (a) the sources of information, (b) snap and systematic judgments, (c) attributions, and (d) cognitive distortions (Weiten & Lloyd, 2006).

Sources of Information

Every day we are bombarded with sensory input about the people we encounter. To manage this quantity of data that determines how we react, we use various sources and types of information to categorize the data and form impressions of others. Many times this categorization occurs very quickly, and often, we do not even know that we are forming impressions (Winslow, n.d.). We believe that we are seeing people as they really are. The sources of impression formation include appearance, verbal behavior, actions, nonverbal messages, and information about situations. For example, you are meeting a client for the first time in the client's home. A scantily clad woman with vivid makeup and bleached blonde hair (appearance) opens the door. She says, "Who are you? What do you want?" (verbal). You see her holding a small child very tightly in her arms; she is frowning at the child (nonverbal). Before you have a chance to answer, she slams the door in your face (action). This is a home visit and the client's name is on the mailbox by the door; you are investigating an alleged child abuse reported by the next-door neighbor (situation). In this example, each of the sources of data exists; appearance, verbal and nonverbal messages, and actions add information about the situation. What type of impression did you form of this woman?

Let's look at how we form snap and systematic judgments as we meet individuals for the first time and then as we encounter these individuals again.

Snap and Systematic Judgments

As we form impressions of others, we use snap judgments to record our first impressions. Unless there is a strong motivation to go beyond these first impressions, we often retain them (Sherman, Stroessner, Conrey, & Omar, 2005). Because each of us has so much information to process, we become "cognitive misers." This means that we depend upon automatic processing to summarize and make judgments of others. With automatic processing, we make impressions quickly; these impressions come from many of our previous experiences of other people.

There is another way to process this information by using controlled processing or taking your time to identify their first impressions and consciously move beyond them (Neuberg & Fiske, 1987). Controlled processing is time consuming and difficult. It includes thinking about whether the categories and opinions you are using to make judgments about others are accurate. It is easy if the information you receive fits your traditional way of thinking. But if the information challenges your first impressions, then you have to gather additional information and come up with new categories. This is hard work.

Without this type of intentional reflection, individuals move beyond their quick opinions and begin to make systematic judgments of others. Think about your first impressions of the woman at the door described in the preceding section.

- ◆ Describe her in three words.
- ◆ What was her reaction to you?
- ◆ Why did she react as she did?
- ◆ What was her relationship to the child?
- ◆ Why was she holding the child so tightly?

If you can generate more than one answer to each of these questions, it is easier to move beyond initial assumptions and determine what information you need to understand this woman at a deeper level.

Another way in which we form impression of others is using attribution or ascribing causes for an individual's behavior or situation. We use attribution to make assumptions of why individuals behave the way they do.

Attributions

When we make attributions, we assume we know the causes of another's behavior. These attributions contribute to how we form impressions of others. Sometimes we believe that individuals are responsible for their own behavior. Other times we believe individuals are victims of their environments (Adams & Betz, 1993). For example, as you think about the scantily clad woman described earlier, do you believe that her dress is her own responsibility? Or did another individual or a social norm "cause" her to dress in that fashion? If you believe that she is responsible for her dress, then you ascribe internal attribution, believing that she chooses to dress and act the way she does because of her personality, characteristics, or abilities. If you believe she is responsible for herself, then you think she must accept the consequences for her actions. If you believe that her dress and behavior is not only her personal responsibility, but that she also is under social pressure to dress and act in a certain way, then you ascribe external attribution. In other words, the responsibility for her action and behavior does not just rest with her, but with society.

The "fundamental attribution error" (Gilbert & Malone, 1995) occurs when we tend to explain the behavior of others using personal rather than situational or contextual causes, without knowing the facts. In other words, behavior is a choice of the individual and is influenced by personal characteristics such as temperament, personality, traits, values, and interests. A description of the woman who slammed the door, based upon the fundamental attribution error, might include many of the following comments:

Boy, is she dressing to get attention. She must have a need to be noticed and must be trying to dress provocatively to gain the attention of the men she encounters. The way that she slammed the door means that she knows exactly who I am and why I am here. She does not want me to come in and question her about her behavior to her child. She was holding the child too tightly and she looks like she was trying to hurt the child.

This account does not take into consideration any situational factors such as the reasons she is dressing as she is, her knowledge of the helper's visit, any previous visits she has had from strangers, what happened in the house before she heard the knock on the door, and reasons for holding the child tightly.

Ascribing reasons for behaviors or circumstances without information is likely to cause errors in how we form impressions of others. Cognitive distortion is another way in which we may form erroneous impressions.

Cognitive Distortions

As stated earlier, many times we process information about others quickly; we often lack the motivation to pay attention to details and to question what these details mean. Cognitive distortions occur when we take an easy way to define others by using social categorization and stereotyping. Social categorization occurs when we define others as "them" or "us." By categorizing according to nationality, race, ethnicity, religion, age, gender, sexual orientation, and other groups, we quickly assign characteristics to individuals in those groups. And, if it looks like an individual is not in our group, then he or she immediately falls into the group of "the other." In other words, those who are not similar to us become part of the "out" group. Members of our "in" group have very positive characteristics and are viewed in a favorable light. Those in the "out" group are different and have more negative characteristics. Let's return to the woman answering the door. In what ways does she belong to "your" group or groups? In what ways is she different? Would you consider her to be part of the "out" group or the "in" group? Why?

Stereotyping is another way we create cognitive distortions. When we stereotype others, we immediately ascribed characteristics just because they belong to a certain group. Phrases such as "all women," "most men," "Catholics are," and "Hispanics always" denote stereotyping. Many stereotypic beliefs that we hold are not obvious to us. In fact, we confuse stereotypes with facts. How do we know when we are using stereotypic or factual thinking? One signal occurs when we are surprised by the behavior of others. When was the last time you were pleased when an elderly man or woman competed and won a physically based sporting event or someone with a serious mental illness was able to maintain stable employment? The surprise you felt indicates that that individual violated the norms or stereotypes that you have for a particular group.

Now that you are more familiar with different ways that you form impressions of others and are aware of barriers to that process, let us examine how this knowledge helps you as a case manager engage in assessment and report documenting.

●●●●●●●●●●●●● Exercise 6: Bridget—Is She "In" or "Out"?

1. Read the "Case Study: Bridget, Part 1" and then answer the questions 2 and 3.

●●●●●●●●●●●●● Case Study: Bridget, Part 1

Bridget is 22 years old and a drug addict. Her parents were divorced in her early teens. She changed high schools three times. Her father is an alcoholic and her mother is clinically depressed. She has been in jail nine times and she has been in and out of hospitals for the past five years with various illnesses. Her boyfriend physically abuses her. For the past three years, Bridget has been involved in illegal activities to get money for drugs or to get drugs. Right now she is a convicted felon, and she could receive a sentence of six months in the penitentiary or six months on probation. She wrote bad checks and was caught with drug paraphernalia. Bridget has just found out that she is pregnant with a girl. She does not know who the father is.

Bridget has a brother and two sisters. She grew up in a suburban neighborhood. In her early teens, her dad admitted that he was an alcoholic. He left home to "get some help" but never came back. He divorced Bridget's mother two years later. The family had to move out of the neighborhood into a smaller house. They had to move again to a house that charged less rent. Changing schools with each move, Bridget began to use drugs to help her belong to an "in" crowd.

2. What are your first quick impressions of Bridget based upon her appearance, verbal behavior, actions, nonverbal messages, and information about the situation?

_____

_____

_____

3. Why do you think you made those first quick impressions?

_____

_____

_____

4. Read the "Case Study: Bridget, Part 2" and then answer the questions 5 and 6.

•••••••••••••• ● Case Study: Bridget, Part 2

Bridget moved out of her mother's house during her senior year and moved in with her father. Bridget's father was dating every night and he knew only a little about what Bridget was doing. She was using drugs daily, including marijuana, cocaine, and crystal meth—and she was now living with her boyfriend. Bridget worked at a local grocery store. Her boyfriend was selling and using drugs. Bridget attended school sporadically. She graduated and passed the local and state tests. After graduation, she continued living with her boyfriend. Her work record was irregular and she kept changing jobs.

At the age of 20, Bridget and her boyfriend traveled to Mexico to buy drugs. Their plan was to buy the drugs and then sell them in the United States. Bridget made the trip to Mexico successfully. But on the return trip, she was stopped by the police just after she crossed the border. She was jailed for possession. She called her family, but they decided that they would leave her in jail for one night. Bridget was released on bail. Her boyfriend was already out of jail on bail. They found their car and unloaded the drugs that the police did not find. She was arrested soon after that, but she had a false I.D. The police ran the I.D., discovered who she was, and then arrested her again.

5. What are your more systematic judgments of Bridget?

_____

_____

_____

6. How have these changed from your first impressions? Why do you think that these impressions changed?

_____

_____

_____

7. Read the "Case Study: Bridget, Part 3" and then answer the questions 8 and 9.

·············● Case Study: Bridget, Part 3

Bridget stayed out of jail for three months. She then was arrested for prostitution. This time she spent almost four months in jail. She was placed on probation and lived in a halfway house. During that time she received a chip in Alcoholics Anonymous for 100 days of sobriety. Bridget decided that she would move back home, so she began to live with her mother. She got a job, paid rent to her mother, and then moved into her apartment. She took her boyfriend back. Before long, she began using drugs again. Her boyfriend continued his physical abuse. She lost her job for irregular attendance and spent her money on drugs. That summer Bridget was hospitalized with pneumonia. Her physical health had deteriorated. She weighed only 90 pounds, and she had lost most of her hair and some of her teeth. While she was in the hospital many of her family came to visit. They all wanted to help her. Bridget refused. All that she could think about was going back to her boyfriend and the drugs.

8. Do you think that Bridget is responsible for her situation (internal attribution) or is her environment responsible? Explain the rationale for your answer.

_____

_____

_____

9. How does "fundamental attribution error" apply to your thoughts about Bridget?

_____

_____

_____

10. Read the "Case Study: Bridget, Part 4" and then answer the questions 11, 12 and 13.

·············● Case Study: Bridget, Part 4

Once Bridget was out of the hospital, she moved in with two friends. Her boyfriend joined her there. She continued to use drugs. She stole checks, food, and medicine. Bridget sold the drugs that she didn't use. She was arrested again. In the jail, she tried to commit suicide. The police took her to the hospital. She was placed on suicide watch. During a routine physical exam, Bridget found out that she was pregnant. She waited three months for a court date. She was placed in rehabilitation for six months and on probation for three years. It is clear that if she violates the law again, she will go to prison.

Currently Bridget is four months pregnant and has no idea who the father of her child is. She is in rehabilitation. Her mother comes to visit her. Right now she is clean.

11. To which social categories does Bridget belong? To which social categories do you belong?

_____

_____

12. In what ways is Bridget in your "in" group and your "out" group? How does this influence your impressions of her and how would this influence your initial assessment of her?

_____

_____

_____

13. Did you or could you stereotype Bridget after reading the first two paragraphs? Describe the stereotype? After knowing a more complete story, does the stereotype remain?

_____

_____

_____

⬤ Self-Assessment

The following activity will help you assess what you have learned from Chapter 4. Focus on what you understand and what additional information would help you expand your knowledge about the assessment phase of case management.

1. How will knowledge about forming impressions of others influence your work as a case manager?

_____

_____

_____

2. Select one client from your *Generalist Case Management* text or this chapter, and describe how you would use information about forming impressions of others, snap and systematic judgments, attribution, and cognitive distortions to conduct an intake interview and record case notes of that interview.

_____

_____

_____

3. List the questions that remain for you after reading Chapter 4 of *Generalist Case Management*.

_____

_____

_____

_____

Pretest Answers

1. Structured interviews are direct and focused and are guided by a set of specific questions that elicit information to gain a brief overview of the problem and the context (p. 87). Unstructured interviews use questions that arise from conversation; they are broad, and reflective and encourage sharing information to develop rapport (p. 88).

2. The case manager explains and confirms the client's desire for services, records information, identifies the next steps, informs the client of eligibility requirements, and clarifies what the agency can legally provide. Also the helper and the client define needs and problems, identify strengths and resources, and begin the helping relationship (p. 84).

3. The individual becomes a client after the intake interview, if the eligibility criteria were met and the client agrees to receive services.

4. Case assignment occurs (1) when the intake interviewer assigns the case to a case manager, (2) a specialized worker analyzes the complexities of the case, and/or (3) a team of professionals meets to begin work with each other and with the client on the client's behalf (p. 92).

References

Adams, E. M., & Betz, N. E. (1993). Gender differences in counselor attitudes toward and attribution about incest. *Journal of Counseling Psychology, 40*(2), 210–216.

Gilbert, D. T., & Malone, P. S. (1995). The correspondence bias. *Psychological Bulletin, 117,* 21–38.

Homeless Education Program. (n.d.). *Case study 1: Homeless liaison networking session.* Retrieved December 11, 2005, from http://www.utdanacenter.org/theo/pdffiles/Abilene_Case_Studies.pdf.

Neuberg, S. L., & Fiske, S. T. (1987). Motivational influences on impressions formation: Outcome dependency, accuracy-driven attention, and individuating processes. *Journal of Personality and Social Psychology, 53*(3), 431–444.

Sherman, J. W., Stroessner, S. J., Conrey, F. R., & Omar, A. (2005). Prejudice and stereotype maintenance processes: Attention, attribution, and individuation. *Journal of Personality and Social Psychology, 89*(4), 607–622.

Weiten, W., & Lloyd, M. A. (2006). *Psychology applied to modern life: Adjustment in the 21st century* (8th ed.). Belmont, CA: Wadsworth.

Winslow, M. (n.d.). *Social perception.* Retrieved December 11, 2005, from http://people.eku.edu/winslowm/psy300/if-attributionhandout. pdf.

Effective Intake Interviewing

The intake interview, the focus of Chapter 5 in *Generalist Case Management*, begins the case management process. During this initial meeting, the case manager and the applicant reach an understanding of the applicant's problems and their context. The case manager also learns about the applicant. The attitudes and characteristics of the interviewer coupled with communication skills contribute to the successful first encounter between the case manager and the applicant. The following exercises provide ways for you to develop your understanding of intake interviewing and to practice the skills it requires.

⬤ Pretest

When you finish reading Chapter 5 in *Generalist Case Management*, answer the following questions and complete the items.

1. List ways that the attitudes of the case manager affect the interview process.

_____

_____

_____

2. What are the important physical characteristics of the setting where the interview occurs?

_____

_____

_____

3. Describe three important interviewing skills.

_____

_____

_____

4. Why is questioning an art?

_____

_____

_____

5. Identify two pitfalls related to intake interviewing.

_____

_____

_____

⬤ Chapter Summary

During the initial interview, the case manager should strive to communicate a helping attitude toward the client. This may be accomplished by being sensitive to the needs of the client and communicating warmth, acceptance, and genuineness. The case manager also needs to be sensitive to issues of diversity, such as race, gender, sexual orientation, religion, ability, and age. During the initial interview, the communication skills of the case manager are critical in developing a positive relationship with the applicant. Using language that the applicant can understand, showing congruence between verbal and nonverbal messages, and practicing active listening all contribute to relationship development. Listening involves more than just hearing what the applicant says verbally. The case manager's behavior should also include attending to the nonverbal messages of the applicant, keeping an open posture and a comfortable distance, maintaining appropriate eye contact, and staying relaxed.

In addition to communication skills, the physical setting of the interview can also encourage positive interactions during the initial interview. The interview should occur in an area that will ensure confidentiality, remove any potential physical barriers, and reduce the likelihood of disruptions. Lastly, the case manager should make every effort to avoid solving problems prematurely, giving advice, relying excessively on closed questions, or rushing to fill silences during the interview.

● Exercise 1: Attitudes and Characteristics of Interviewers

During an interview, the case manager demonstrates attitudes of the self and other. One way to learn about these attitudes and characteristics is to watch others conduct interviews.

1. Select two television programs that include interviews; for example, *News Hour* (PBS), the Sunday morning network news shows, and talk shows such as *Larry King Live* and *Oprah*. Watch interview segments that last approximately five minutes.

2. Describe the following:

   Settings: _____

   _____

   _____

   _____

   Interviewees: _____

   _____

   _____

   _____

   Interviewers: _____

   _____

   _____

   _____

3. Compare the interview styles: greeting, questioning, control, and climate.

   _____

   _____

   _____

   _____

   _____

   _____

4. What did you like or dislike about each interview?

   _____

   _____

   _____

   _____

   _____

   _____

● Exercise 2: When I Was the "Stranger"

The purpose of this exercise is to help you identify what it is like to be different or to be a "stranger" in a specific environment. Answering the following questions will help you identify and explore that experience.

1. Describe a time when you felt you were different, a "stranger," or an outcast.

_____

_____

_____

2. How did you react in this situation? How did you feel?

_____

_____

_____

3. What did you think others were communicating to you?

_____

_____

_____

4. What did you communicate to them?

_____

_____

_____

● Exercise 3: Developing Cultural Sensitivities

Review the section on cultural sensitivity in Chapter 5 in *Generalist Case Management*.

1. Several potential client groups are discussed. With which one would you be least comfortable?

_____

_____

_____

2. Describe a scenario where you are conducting an intake interview with a client in this particular client group.

_____

_____

_____

3. Identify three reasons that you will have difficulty interviewing this client.

_____

_____

_____

_____

4. Put yourself in the client's place and describe the client's thoughts prior to coming in for the interview.

_____

_____

_____

_____

_____

5. Answer the following questions about your description of the client's point of view.

• What was the experience of writing as if you were the client like for you?

_____

_____

_____

• What have you learned from this experience about your own cultural sensitivity?

_____

_____

_____

Exercise 4: Using Language the Client Understands

The following quote is a case manager's explanation of the services available and the purpose of the interview.

1. Read the following remarks at the beginning of an intake interview:

I am glad that you are here today. I want to tell you about our services that we may be able to offer you. First is the Bridges program. It provides a case manager and vouchers, and you become part of our Helpers program. If you are able to work through Phase One: Learning and Developing Skills, then you will be eligible for Phase Two. In Phase Two, we will develop your case in multiple ways so that you can be an applicant for Phase Three. Now Phase Three is for your whole family except for the members who do not qualify and fall into our Non-Standard category. We have criteria for each of these phases.

Now that you have a summary, I am going to ask you some questions.

2. Review the case manager's statement. It is not very clear, is it? Review the statement and circle all of the phases that you believe might have been unclear to the client. For each item circled, suggest an alternative statement that presents the information about the agency and its services more clearly.

_____

_____

_____

_____

● Exercise 5: Active Listening Exercise

Using active listening or attending behavior with a client is one way to communicate to the client that he or she is important. Using various gestures and nonverbal signals, the case manager allows the client to choose the path of the conversation while paying attention to the message the client is conveying.

1. Select a friend who is willing to help you.

2. Ask the friend to talk to you about an event, situation, or problem he or she does not mind sharing. Find a quiet spot so that the two of you are not interrupted.

3. Use the SOLER behaviors presented in your text as you listen to your friend talk.

4. After you have practiced your active listening, describe to your friend what it was like to listen using this technique. Then ask your friend to share his or her experience.

Your experiences

_____

_____

_____

_____

_____

Your friend's experiences

_____

_____

_____

_____

_____

● Exercise 6: Questioning Activity

Chapter 5 in *Generalist Case Management* describes five situations when questions are appropriate and relevant.

1. Review the five situations.

2. Practice your questioning skills by formulating five appropriate questions for each of the following case examples.

Case 1

Brigitta is an angry, frustrated client who has been living on her own with her two young sons in community housing for over a year. She believes the feelings she is experiencing are a reaction to her mother constantly calling her, asking her to come by, and wanting her to account for her time. She decides to see a human service professional because she is at the end of her rope. As the helper explores this situation with Brigitta, however, she discovers that Brigitta's father died six months ago. Her mother is lonely and mourning, and Brigitta, who moved out three months before he died, feels guilty not only about moving out but also about not returning home when her mother needs her.

To begin the interview: _____

_____

_____

To elicit specific information: _____

_____

To focus the client's attention: _____

_____

_____

To clarify: _____

_____

_____

To identify client strengths: _____

_____

_____

Case 2

Rena has always had a problem with obesity. She has had diabetes since she was 11 and has fought her overweight condition and high blood pressure since she was a teenager. She starts each new diet with great enthusiasm, but she soon returns to her old eating habits. Rena is beginning a new diet developed by a leading movie star, and she has great hopes. She tries not to remember the 400 pounds she has lost and regained in the past 10 years.

To begin the interview: _____

_____

_____

To elicit specific information: _____

_____

_____

To focus the client's attention: _____

_____

_____

To clarify: _____

_____

_____

To identify client strengths: _____

_____

_____

Case 3

Jim joined a smoking cessation group at the medical center a month ago. As all participants do initially, Jim told the group about his tobacco habit and stated that his wife was adamant that he quit. He and his wife became parents for the first time two months ago, and she fears the effects of smoke on the baby. It was only last night, though, that Jim shared with the group his worries about beginning a topical precancerous treatment on his face and about his baby's lack of response to stimuli.

To begin the interview: _____

_____

_____

To elicit specific information: _____

_____

_____

To focus the client's attention: _____

_____

_____

To clarify: _____

_____

_____

To identify client strengths: _____

_____

_____

···········•• Exercise 7: Responding

After reading the following examples, write three different responses: a paraphrase, a clarification, and an open-ended question.

<u>Helping Situation 1</u>

I can't seem to keep my mind on my work these days. I forget what I am doing, I find myself staring out the window, my kids keep yelling at me, I can't get my work completed. I know that my boss is not pleased with me. I'm not pleased with myself. Everyone is giving me a hard time. I don't sleep very well. I am a mess.

Paraphrase: _____

_____

_____

Clarification: _____

_____

_____

Open-Ended Question: _____

_____

_____

Helping Situation 2

My momma told me that I had to come to see you. My teacher found out that I was coming, and she told me to tell you what I knew about my dad. I am not sure what to say. My daddy loves me. He says that he loves me special.

Paraphrase: _____

_____

_____

Clarification: _____

_____

_____

Open-Ended Question: _____

_____

_____

Helping Situation 3

I am not sure what the problem is (pause). . . .I just don't know. . . .

Paraphrase: _____

_____

_____

Clarification: _____

_____

_____

Open-Ended Question: _____

_____

_____

Helping Situation 4

Our mom and dad are not doing too well. Mom cannot dress herself anymore, and she needs help to prepare her food. She cannot remember what day it is, forgets to take her medicines, and does not know many of her friends. Dad is taking care of her as best as he can, but his abilities are limited, too. He is worn out from caring for her, and he does not have time to do anything for himself. We are crazy from worry.

Paraphrase: _____

_____

_____

Clarification: _____

_____

_____

Open-Ended Question: _____

_____

_____

⬤ In More Depth: Talking to Children

There are multiple ways that case managers provide services to children in need either by supporting families who have children with special needs or working directly with children. Children begin the case management process with an intake interview, much the same way as adults do. Many case managers indicate that, while they serve children, they gather information from other sources such as parents, school officials, and written case records. Ultimately, most case managers also want to hear from the child. Children have physical, cognitive, and social developmental characteristics; because they are a unique population, special knowledge, skills, and values are required to conduct this first interview.

This chapter provides information on the characteristics of children between the ages 6 and 12, what psychologists label middle childhood, and presents guidelines for talking with these children, especially for the first time in the intake interview. This age range is a unique time in a child's life; "Keep in mind that the school child's head is not where yours is. It's not just a matter of physical growth—it's perhaps more a matter of intellectual change—the fact that their intellectual feet are still not firmly grounded. Too, their heads may be closer to the clouds. And perhaps that's why they see magic more clearly than we adults do" (LeFrancois, 2001, p. 374).

Let's look at the physical, cognitive, and social development for children in middle childhood, as well as problems or challenges they may experience.

Physical Growth

There are physical measures important to note in children in middle childhood. A marked growth spurt occurs as girls, on average, gain more weight and height. Both girls and boys decrease their fatty mass as their bone and muscle develop; this trend is consistent with good nutrition. Children also continue to develop their fine and gross motor skills. The increase in physical abilities allows them to expand their interest in creative efforts and sports requiring coordination and physical strength. Obesity emerges as a problem for many children this age due to overeating (Lamerez, Kuepper, & Bruning, 2005), poor nutrition, lack of physical activity (Weiten & Lloyd, 2006), cultural or psychological factors, such as using food as a reward or a punishment, and genetic factors (Malina & Bouchard, 1991). Other physical problems are sensory related such as visual or hearing impairments and disease-related difficulties linked to such diseases as muscular dystrophy and diabetes.. Children are also reaching puberty at younger ages. This change in physical maturation is problematic because cognitive and social development remain the same.

Cognitive Development

Two important concepts help explain cognitive development in middle childhood: the use of concrete operations and intelligence. Children who are able to think concretely demonstrate skills such as engaging in conversations, performing reversible thinking, using rules of logic, and understanding concepts based upon concrete objects or their past experiences (Piaget, 1960). Children have conversations; they engage in dialogue, listen, and respond appropriately. They take turns in conversation and demonstrate an interest in others. The following conversation between two 7-year-olds during school playtime illustrates a typical conversation:

Suzie: Can I have your hammer?
Jorge: I am using it.
Suzie: What are you making?

Jorge: A puzzle with this wood.
Suzie: Okay. But I want the hammer.
Jorge: Not now. I am busy.

Children also perform reversible thinking; this means that they may have an idea or understanding and then change that understanding. The following conversation illustrates the change of thinking when Paula, age 9, discusses the subject of ghosts with her mom. Note that her mother uses a concrete illustration of a ghost, instead of an abstract idea.

Paula: Are you scared during Halloween? I mean if I am a ghost.
Mom: Is there something that makes you feel scared?
Paula: Ms. Brewer at school says that after Halloween all of the ghosts will disappear.
Mom: Paula, let me show you what she means. See this ghost that I made for the door. After tonight I will take it down and put it away. Here let me show you. (Mom takes the ghost down and puts it away and shuts the closet where she puts it.)
Paula: But I think that I will disappear.
Mom: Here let's practice putting on your costume and then taking it off and putting it away. (They do this). There, now you know that disappearing ghosts means putting away decorations and costumes.
Paula: Can I make the kitty disappear?
Mom: Well, the kitty can go outside and you will not be able to see her. But we still have to take care of her. She is still there.

Because children are beginning to use logic, they can use it to make sense of their world. They also have the ability to use rules of logic to construct knowledge. In the conversation above, Paula is learning about the concept of disappear. Because it is an abstract concept, her mom uses concrete examples to explain what the concept disappear means, as it relates to her "being a ghost" for Halloween. Paula uses a rule of logic to extend the concept of disappear to the kitty. In this example, her mother must help Paula understand that the rules of logic for the ghost disappearing do not apply to the kitty.

Mom: Paula, let the kitty out. Now has the kitty disappeared?
Paula: I know where she is. When she goes out, she has a favorite place to sleep in the sun.
Mom: Why don't you check and see if the kitty is there? (Paula checks).
Paula: Yup, she's there.
Mom: Has she disappeared?
Paula: Nope. I can't see her from the window, but I know where she is.

Children from 6 to 12 years of age recall information from the past. They display long-term memory as they ride a bicycle, play video games, and make baskets at the free-throw line during a basketball game. As children tell stories about themselves or recall specific actions from the past, they show their autobiographical memory (Brouillet & Lepine, 2005).

Intelligence provides another way professionals consider children's cognitive abilities. One theory is that intelligence is a quality or a measure of functioning and is based upon characteristics or traits. General intelligence focuses abilities that are innate within the individual and include solving problems, reasoning, and analyzing. Specific intelligence includes abilities such as knowledge of vocabulary, general information, and arithmetic skills (Engle, Tuholski, Laughlin, & Conway, 1999). Another way of viewing intelligence is by seeing how individuals adapt to the world. This approach, called successful intelligence, considers the context of intelligence and the control of the environment. This means that children choose the environments in which they function and then change them (Sternberg, 1998). Children demonstrate successful intelligence as they choose their friends, change their social interactions from setting to setting, and decide what they do in their spare time.

Consideration of multiple intelligences also focuses on the ways that we adapt to our environment. These include linguistic, musical, logical-mathematical, spatial, bodily-kinesthetic, and personal traits or characteristics that we use to operate and focus in the world (Gardner, 1998). The intelligences point out individual differences and underscore the value of multiple approaches to understanding and functioning in the world.

Understanding a child's intelligence may help a case manager prepare for an initial contact with a child. A child's written case file may contain scores from more traditional intelligence tests such as the Wechsler

Intelligence Scale for Children (WISC). Alternative information about successful intelligence or multiple intelligence may be gained during the initial interview and may help the case manager choose ways in which to communicate and establish rapport. Often professionals use tests to determine the intelligence of children. Chapter 6 in *Generalist Case Management* addresses the use of tests to measure specific traits. There is also a caution about how to use test results in interpreting what we know about clients. This caution applies equally to the children case managers test.

Understanding about intellectual exceptionality in children helps case managers to note special needs, such as mental retardation, learning disabilities, intellectual giftedness, and creativity. Information about each of these exceptionalities follows. The degree of mental retardation defines a child's ability to learn and to adapt to the environment. This exceptionality includes a depressed intellectual functioning and a limitation in levels of independence, social responsibility, and social effectiveness. Children who are developmentally delayed are not mentally retarded; their late development is attributed to language difficulties, illness, or other factors.

Another exceptionality related to cognitive development is the diagnosis of learning disabilities and includes a variety of conditions. The Individuals with Disabilities Act (IDEA) helps define this category: (a) disparity between expected and actual behavior; (b) uneven pattern of achievement; (c) problems in psychological process related to reading or arithmetic; (d) problems not resulting from vision or hearing impairments or mental retardation (National Center for Learning Disabilities, 2005). Symptoms of children with learning disabilities include difficulty with reading and writing tasks, poor memory, difficulty maintaining attention, motor problems, slow work pace, difficulty in understanding concrete or abstract concepts, and difficulty following instructions (National Center for Learning Disabilities, 2005).

Intellectually gifted and creative children also have specific difficulties in school and at home. Giftedness, defined by IDEA, means children who have outstanding abilities and are capable of high performance. Children with this exceptionality often have a difficult time relating to their peers, are more comfortable with older children and adults, have a more sophisticated grasp of the language, read widely, and have a variety of interests. Children who are creative demonstrate skills of divergent thinking, represented in their abilities to produce a wide variety of solutions to problems, switch from one solution to the next, and develop unique approaches to solving problems. Because gifted and creative children are not challenged in the traditional school environment, they also can manifest behavior problems and/or become social isolates.

Social Development

Areas of social cognition, self-esteem, and relationships represent the social development of children in middle childhood. From the age of 6 until 12, children change how they view themselves in relation to others. Children begin to see that others have a point of view, but also believe others would change to theirs if they knew what it was. They then change to a self-reflective point of view where they acknowledge their own and others' points of view. Finally, they adopt a mutual point of view (Selman, 1980; LeFrancois, 2001). Once they understand the points of view of others, they may be willing to consider differences, express empathy, and facilitate self-change. The mutual point of view is just beginning to develop during the latter stages of middle childhood.

Understanding the self-esteem of children provides case managers with information about children and how they feel about their competencies and self-worth. Children usually have a general sense of their over all worth. Then they judge themselves according to specific competencies such as their scholastic ability, athletic competence, social acceptance, behavioral conduct, and physical appearance (Harter, 1987). Judgments about self-worth are founded on how children would like to be and how they believe others view them. The opinions of parents, influential adults, and friends are most important (Fordham & Stevenson-Hinde, 1999). Physical appearance is often one of the most important areas (Harter, 1987). Self-worth is linked to self-concept, emotion and mood, and motivation (Chapman & Mullis, 1999). A positive sense of self-worth is related to a good self-concept, happiness, and self-efficacy. A negative sense of self-worth is related to low self-concept, unhappiness, and depression.

Friendships become increasingly important during middle childhood, especially in the preteen years. Best friends and a circle of friends contribute to the social development of the child. Five categories of social status describe the different experiences children have with friendships. The "sociometric stars" are liked by a majority of their peers. The "mixers" interact often with their peers; some are well-liked and some are not. The "teacher negatives" experience conflicts with their teachers; some are liked and some are not. The "tuned out" are less involved with peers and ignored. The "sociometric rejectees" are not liked very much (Gottman, 1977). If a child is rejected by peers, reactions include anger, retaliation, and aggression (Henington, Hugs, Cavell, & Thompson, 1998). Children without friends suffer from depression, bullying, and loneliness.

Victimization of children is a serious problem that affects a child's growth and development. There are several types of victimization (Finkelhor & Dziuba-Leatherman, 1994). Pandemic victimization describes the occasional suffering related to growing up such as sibling assault, peers assault, and other crimes. Extraordinary victimization refers to high-profile kidnapping or violent crime. Acute victimization includes physical abuse, neglect, emotional maltreatment, medical neglect, and sexual abuse, and it is fairly prevalent in our society (U.S. Bureau of the Census, 1998). There are physical and psychological consequences of acute victimization, such as emotional withdrawal, aggressiveness, truancy, delinquency, poor school achievement, and poor social relationships.

Before we introduce ideas about how to talk with children in middle childhood, let's explore information about child development that might be helpful to you.

 # Exercise 8: Considering James and Samantha

1. List the facts that you believe are most relevant to you as you conduct an intake interview with children ages 6 to 12.

Physical Development

_____

_____

_____

_____

Cognitive Development

_____

_____

_____

_____

Social Development

_____

_____

_____

_____

2. Re-read the case of James and Samantha in Chapter 4 of this workbook.

James and Samantha

James is 10 years old and his sister, Samantha, is 8. Both attended Boone Elementary School and lived with their aunt and uncle; their parents are in prison. In the middle of the school year, the aunt told the children that they were going to move that evening. They picked up their clothes and a few toys and moved into a shelter. They didn't know that this was a shelter for women and children who were being abused. The children were brokenhearted to leave their school. They had good friends there. Samantha says that she understands why she needs to go to another school, but James is angry that he has to transfer. Finally, the staff at the shelter tried to work out transportation back to the school, but school officials told the children's aunt that they could not transfer back into the old district. The school counselor has referred James and Samantha to you.

3. Review the child development facts that you listed in Question 1. How would each of those facts help you interview James and Samantha? Add any facts that you did not list for Question 1.

Physical Development

_____

_____

_____

_____

Cognitive Development

_____

_____

_____

_____

Social Development

_____

_____

_____

_____

Now that you have studied child development for children in middle childhood, let's look at guidelines for talking with children in this stage of development.

Guidelines for the Intake Interview

Case managers who are beginning their work with young clients often need to shift their thinking from "working with clients" to "working with children." Many times when a professional uses the term "client," an adult male or female comes to mind. Because of their age and lack of experience, working with children requires special care and consideration. There is an immediate power differential because young children are taught to have respect for adults, especially for those in authority. Children are involved in a developmental process; successful case managers consider where the child is in the developmental framework and begin case management with the child's ability and level of development in mind.

Getting Ready for the Intake Interview

In some ways, beginning the intake interview occurs before the child comes to the office or before the case manager visits the child. The case manager prepares the physical space to make the child comfortable. This preparation also helps the case manager establish rapport. Here are some guidelines to follow when preparing the room in which the intake interview will take place (Thompson, Rudolph, & Henderson, 2004).

✦ Provide a relaxed atmosphere. This means use comfortable chairs and tables that are child size and child friendly. Set the furniture so the child can be face-to-face with you and not have to look up.

✦ Provide an atmosphere that is bright and not too cluttered. Children love bright colors and decorations with animals, dolls, and animated characters with which they are familiar.

✦ Establish a spacious atmosphere. Leave open space in the room. Do not put a desk or table between you and the child.

✦ Provide a barrier that the child can use to create a safe distance from you. This means that the child can choose where to put the chair or can hold a pillow or a blanket—or can move a table between you and him or her.

✦ Have toys, drawing material, desk, and dolls that might help facilitate conversation. You will use these materials to involve the child in activities. Usually case managers gain information as the child draws, paints, role plays or the like. Even preteens may want to use art or music to talk about their situations rather than just engage in conversation. Also, games and other materials indicate to children that your space is a good place for them.

These suggestions are still relevant if the case manager is meeting the child or the family at the home. Sometimes the case manager can talk with the family about arranging a special room for the meeting, indicating that a place where the child would be comfortable is optimal.

The child may be nervous at the first interview. At the very least, children may have questions about case management and what is expected of them. Children often have questions that differ from those of adults. Many times children do not have a choice about receiving case management services. Even though the case manager, and perhaps the parents, knows that the child will benefit from case management services, the child does not understand this. Here are some questions children may have (Thompson, Rudolph, & Henderson, 2004).

✦ What is case management?
✦ Why do I have to do this?
✦ What's wrong with me?
✦ Will this hurt? Will I get a shot? Medicine?
✦ Do I have to go?
✦ Do I have to do this just once?
✦ What do I do?

These questions indicate fear of a new situation, talking to a stranger, and answering questions and not understanding case management and the need for it. You must be able to answer these questions using language that children can understand. Here are some ways to approach these questions:

Child: What is case management?
Case Manager: I am a case manager. My job is to help you. I am going to . . .
Child: Why do I have to do this?
Case Manager: People who care about you think I could help you.
Child: What's wrong with me?
Case Manager: I don't think anything is wrong. My work is to get others to help you.
Child: Will this hurt? Will I get a shot? Medicine?
Case Manager: I will not hurt you. Today we are going to talk and play. I want to know you better.
Child: Do I have to go?
Case Manager: I am not sure where you will go. If you have to go anywhere, someone you know will go with you.
Child: Do I have to do this just once?
Case Manager: You and I will see each other today. Then we will decide what else we need to do.
Child: What do I do?
Case Manager: We can start by drawing this picture. Can you draw your family and your house?

The Focus of the Interview

As discussed earlier, any information that you can learn about the child before the initial interview helps you prepare. Two factors guide your initial interview with the child: the goal of your interview and the information you need to obtain. For example, if you are working with a child who has a chronic illness, you may need to engage the child to establish a relationship, determine how the child is feeling physically, what the child knows about his or her medical situation, and what social/emotional effects the illness has on the child. Of course, other sources of information may include parents and medical staff. Another child may be eligible to receive case mana_____ices because he is living in foster care while his parents are incarcerated. Interviewing this_____e first time, the case manager may focus on the emotional status of the child, comfort with the _____mily, and knowledge of his parent's situation. Additional sources of information may be the department of human services, the public schools, if appropriate, information about the foster parents, and the status of parents in the criminal justice system. Regardless of the situation, the focus of the initial interview is establishing rapport with the child, assessing, exploring what the child currently understands about the situation, understanding the strengths of the child, understanding the fears and concerns of the child, and explaining case management.

The following case lets you use the concepts about how to conduct an intake interview with children in middle childhood.

The Case of Tannie and Lindie

I received a call from Inez Tucker, the principal of the local elementary school in our county. She and I had worked together before on several cases involving students for whom home life is particularly difficult. Since the implementation of "No Child Left Behind," each school in the school district targets students who are in danger of failing and tries to address barriers to their academic success. Often these barriers involve home and neighborhood factors, as well as individual social and emotional problems. Inez asked if she could meet me for lunch, explaining that she had a complicated case that would take about 30 minutes to explain and discuss. I am a child psychologist, but I often serve as a case manager for children who have multiple problems and are not succeeding in school. I am paid through a special grant that the school received from the state to help those students who need services that the school cannot deliver.

I met Inez at our appointed time at a small cafe downtown. The owner saved us a corner table in the back, where we could talk without interruption and without being overheard. Confidentiality is important for both of us. Inez came with only a few notes and started by explaining how difficult this case was for her.

"Two weeks into the school term, a young mother brought her two children, Tannie and Lindie, to school. None of them spoke English. Speaking what we took for a South American Indian dialect, the mother tried to communicate. Three teachers in our school speak fluent Spanish, and two are native speakers. None of them spoke the indigenous dialect. After considerable effort on the part of several of us, including the three Spanish-speaking teachers, to talk with the children and the mother, I asked the custodian to join the conversation. He speaks a mixture of Indian dialect and Spanish. The teacher also asked the children to join the conversation. Although the custodian could not translate exactly what the mother and the children said, he could help us understand some of the conversation."

Inez took out her notes and read to me the following facts that she believes she has learned about this situation.

- ✦ "The children, both girls, are 9 and 10 years of age.
- ✦ The mother and the girls live in a trailer park three blocks from the school.
- ✦ The mother has no job and no income from the family.
- ✦ The mother is a single parent.
- ✦ The mother can neither read nor write.
- ✦ The children can neither read nor write.
- ✦ The family has no permanent records.
- ✦ The children have no immunization records.
- ✦ The children have never attended school."

Inez continued her story: "Since the girls have been coming to school, they have been receiving special tutoring. They go to class in the morning, but after an hour's time, they begin to walk around the classroom. They will not sit down, and they become agitated. The teacher walks them down to my office. I have begun to let them play with toys in my office until the resource teacher comes to get them. She is working to teach them the alphabet, and she is teaching them words that might be useful to them. The girls respond well to this individual attention. They have been in school five weeks now and they have come to school about half of that time. They really don't understand the language, but this is made more difficult because they don't understand the culture of the school.

"I know that there are lots of needs, both for the family and for the girls. And they must have their immunizations if they are to remain in school. But right now I just want to hear from them about how they are doing. I would love to have more information about them, so I can understand what they are going through, how they like school, and what we can do for them."

Inez then asked me if I would interview them. She would like to refer them to me for case management. A referral means that I would set up an interview with them and with the mother. I agreed informally to accept the referral, based upon the information that Inez had provided. I would begin my work with an intake interview.

Two weeks later the official referral was accepted, and I scheduled a time to talk with the girls after gaining the mother's permission to do so. I decided to interview both of them together. Since I would be a stranger to them, I thought that they would be more comfortable meeting with me together. To prepare, I follow three steps: considering current knowledge of the children; considering knowledge of developmental issues; considering use of an interpreter.

·············● Exercise 9: Preparing for the Interview

1. Review the discussion on attitudes and characteristics of interviewers in Chapter 5 of *Generalist Case Management* and the guidelines for interviewing children in this chapter. Assume that you are Tannie and Lindie's case manager. With this information in mind, create a plan for the interview, using the following questions to guide your thinking.

2. Based upon what Inez has told you about the case and what she wishes to know about the girls, what are your goals for this interview with Tannie and Lindie?

_____

_____

_____

_____

3. How will you demonstrate that you are sensitive to Tannie and Lindie's culture?

_____

_____

_____

_____

4. How do you think that Tannie and Lindie feel about the upcoming meeting with you?

_____

_____

_____

_____

5. Describe the ideal setting for the interview.

_____

_____

_____

_____

6. What climate would you like to establish? How will you do so?

_____

_____

_____

_____

7. How will you begin the interview or the greeting?

_____

_____

_____

_____

8. What activities or play will you use in your time with Tannie and Lindie? How does your "approach" help you meet the goals that you established in Question 2?

_____

_____

_____

_____

⬤ Exercise 10: Using Knowledge of Development in Middle Childhood

1. Review the physical, cognitive, and social characteristics that you believe are most relevant for the case manager to remember as she prepares to conduct an intake interview with Tannie and Lindie, ages 9 and 10. Discuss how each characteristic relates to Tannie and Lindie's unique situation and how it will influence the intake interview.

Physical Development

1. _____

_____

2. _____

_____

3. _____

_____

4. _____

_____

Cognitive Development

1. _____

_____

2. _____

_____

3. _____

_____

4. _____

_____

Social Development

1. _____

_____

2. _____

_____

3. _____

_____

4. _____

_____

··············●· Exercise 11: Working with an Interpreter

As you begin to prepare for the interview with Tannie and Lindie, you realize that you will need an interpreter. The likely candidate is the custodian. Because you already speak fluent Spanish and are fairly fluent in French, you have never needed an interpreter. You find an article about interpreters in a professional journal and read it to see if you can discover any guidelines that might help you plan and conduct this interview.

 1. Go to the website that accompanies this book: www.thomsonedu.com/counseling/mcclam, Chapter 5, Link 2. Read the article "Working with Sign Language Interpreters in Human Service Settings." This article will help you understand the role of interpreters. Answer the following questions.

2. What is the role of an interpreter?

_____

_____

_____

3. What does the interpreter NOT do?

_____

_____

_____

_____

4. You will need to ask the custodian if he would be willing to be an interpreter for this intake interview. What will you tell him?

_____

_____

_____

_____

5. Review the plans that you made for the intake interview with Tannie and Lindie in Exercise 9. How does having an interpreter present change those plans?

_____

_____

_____

_____

•••••••••• ● Exercise 12: Intake Summary Sheets

Paperwork is an important part of case management. In this instance, the case manager provides information about Tannie and Lindie to two sources. There is an official school record that is filled out and is part of the official school file. This is Initial Interview Form 440. There is also the Intake Summary Form, which belongs with the case notes prepared for the funding agency.

Assume that you have completed the interview with both Tannie and Lindie, based upon your work in Exercises 9 and 10. Then fill out each of these forms for Lindie, the 10-year-old. You will need to create a profile using the information that you gained from an imaginary intake interview with Lindie.

Date _____

Location of Interview _____

_____

Initial Interview Form 440

1-DEMOGRAPHICS		
NAME:	INFORMANT:	RELATIONSHIP:
NICKNAME:	DATE OF BIRTH:	PLACE OF BIRTH:
AGE:	SEX:	OCCUPATION/SCHOOL:
MARITAL STATUS:	NO. OF SIBLINGS:	PLACE IN BIRTH ORDER:

2-CURRENT LIVING SITUATION

❏ Lives at Home	❏ Lives with Family	❏ Homeless	❏ Foster Home
❏ Residential	❏ Group Home	❏ Boarding Home	❏ Rental
❏ Shelter	❏ State Placement Facility	❏ Friends	❏ Jail

3-EDUCATION

LAST GRADE COMPLETED:	FAVORITE SUBJECTS:	PROBLEM AREAS:

STATED EDUCATIONAL GOALS:

4-EXTRACURRICULAR

HOBBIES and Involvement:

FAVORITE SPORTS and Involvement:

SPARE TIME ACTIVITIES NOW:

WHAT YOU WOULD LIKE TO DO:

5-CASE MANAGEMENT

DOES CLIENT HAVE AN ASSIGNED CASE MANAGER?
❏ YES ❏ NO IF YES, NAME_____

6-PRESENTING PROBLEMS IN CLASSROOM

COMMENTS:

WHY NOW?

7-IMPRESSIONS

Intake Summary

The following data are usually included in an intake recording:

1. Case manager's name, date of the initial contact, and/or the date that the intake summary was prepared.

   _____

   _____

   _____

2. Client's name, address, phone number, and identifying number.

   _____

   _____

   _____

3. The reason for the contact with the client (may also be called the presenting problem).

   _____

   _____

   _____

4. Medical Situation.

   _____

   _____

   _____

5. Family Background. Include names and other information about any family or close friends. Relationships with these people?

   _____

   _____

   _____

6. Living Arrangements. Describe the client's living situation. Where does the client live? What type of facility does client live in? Describe the lifestyle.

   _____

   _____

   _____

7. Economic Information. Amount and source of income and needs.

   _____

   _____

   _____

8. Background Information. Place of birth, ethnic or cultural factors, education, and early history—anything that appears significant in view of the client's current situation, human services planning, and educational planning.

_____

_____

_____

9. Previous contacts with agency (or other agencies).

_____

_____

_____

10. Case manager's impressions/diagnostic summary.

_____

_____

_____

_____

● Self-Assessment

1. Describe the three most important concepts that you learned in this chapter about intake interviewing. Explain why these concepts have meaning for you.

_____

_____

_____

_____

2. What are the challenges you believe you will encounter when conducting an initial intake interview? How will you address these challenges?

_____

_____

_____

_____

3. Imagine that you are conducting an intake interview with a child, age eight. Discuss what information will be important to you as you plan for the interview.

_____

_____

_____

_____

 Pretest Answers

1. The case manager's attitude influences perceptions of the quality of the interview, success or failure of the helping relationship, comfort level of the client, and the amount of the information exchanged (p. 106).

2. The environment must help the case manager ensure confidentiality (quiet and no interruptions), eliminate physical barriers (open layout without desks or tables in between), and promote dialogue (p. 106).

3. Three important interviewing skills are listening (p. 114), questioning (p. 116), and responding (p. 123).

4. Questioning requires a combination of skillful questioning and effective responding. It requires practice (pp. 112 and 116).

5. Pitfalls include prematurely solving problems, giving advice, rushing to fill silences, and relying too much on closed questions (pp. 127–128).

References

Brouillet, P., & Lepine, R. (2005). Working memory and children's use of retrieval to solve addition problems. *Journal of Experimental Child Psychology, 91*(3), 183–204.

Chapman, P. I., & Mullis, R. I. (1999). Adolescent coping strategies and self-esteem. *Child Study Journal, 29*, 66–77.

Engle, R. W., Tuholski, S. W., Laughlin, J. E., & Conway, A. R. A. (1999). Working memory, short-term memory, and general fluid intelligence: A latent-variable approach. *Journal of Experimental Psychology: General, 128*, 309–331.

Finkelhor, D., & Dziuba-Leatherman, J. (1994). Victimization of children. *American Psychologist, 49*, 173–183.

Fordham, K., & Stevenson-Hinde, J. (1999). Shyness, friendship quality, and adjustment during middle childhood. *Journal of Child Psychology & Psychiatry & Allied Disciplines, 40*, 757–768.

Gardner, H. (1998). Are there additional intelligences? The case for naturalist, spiritual, and existential intelligences. In J. Kane (Ed.), *Education, information, and transformation.* Englewood Cliffs, NJ: Prentice-Hall.

Gottman, J. M. (1977). Toward a definition of social isolation in children. *Child Development, 48*, 513–517.

Harter, S. (1987). The determinants and mediational role of global self-worth in children. In N. Eisenberg (Ed.), *Contemporary topics in developmental psychology.* New York: Wiley.

Henington, C., Hugs, J. N., Cavell, T. A., & Thompson, B. (1998). The role of relational aggression in identifying aggressive boys and girls. *Journal of School Psychology, 36*, 457–477.

Lamerez, A., Kuepper, N., & Bruning, N. (2005). Prevalence of obesity, binge eating, and night eating in a cross-sectional field survey of 6-year-old children and their parents in a German urban population. *Journal of Child Psychology and Psychiatry and Allied Disciplines, 46*(4), 385–93.

LeFrancois, G. R. (2001). *Of children* (9th ed.). Belmont, CA: Wadsworth.

Malina, R. M., & Bouchard, C. (1991). Subcutaneous fat distribution during growth. In C. Bouchard & F. D. Johnston (Eds.), *Fat distribution during growth and later health outcomes.* New York: Liss.

National Center for Learning Disabilities. (2005). LD Info Zone. Retreived January 12, 2006, from http://www.ld.org/advocacy/IDEAwatch.cfm.

Piaget, J. (1960). *The child's conception of the world.* London: Routledge.

Selman, R. L. (1980). *The growth of interpersonal understanding.* New York: Academic Press.

Sternberg, R. J. (1998). Applying the triarchic theory of human intelligence in the classroom. In R. J. Sternberg & W. M. Williams (Eds,), *Intelligence, instruction, and assessment: Theory into practice.* Mahwah, NJ: Erlbaum.

Thompson, C., Rudolph, L., & Henderson, D. (2004). *Counseling children.* Pacific Grove, CA: Brooks/Cole.

U.S. Bureau of Census. (1999). *Statistical Abstracts of the United States: 1998* (118th Ed.). Washington, DC: U.S. Government Printing Office.

Weiten, W., & Lloyd, M. A. (2006). *Adjustment in the modern world.* Belmont, CA: Wadsworth.

Chapter 6

Service Delivery Planning

Service delivery is at the heart of case management. Planning occurs before effective and efficient delivery of services and begins with a look back at the assessment phase. Writing a service plan, identifying services, and gathering additional information are all skills that follow. The next exercises will help you develop your planning skills.

 **Pretest**

When you finish reading Chapter 6 in *Generalist Case Management,* answer the following questions and complete the items:

1. Why is it necessary to review the stated problem at the end of the assessment phase?

_____

_____

_____

_____

2. List and describe the parts of a service plan.

_____

_____

_____

_____

3. How would you establish an information and referral system?

_____

_____

_____

_____

4. Compare interviewing and testing as data collection methods.

_____

_____

_____

_____

5. An essential case management planning skill is writing clear goals and objectives. To assist in your review of this skill, read each of the following carefully, circle yes or no, and critique.

   A goal is a brief but broad statement of intent. Are the following statements goals?

   • Improve behavior   YES   NO

   _____

   _____

   • Locate affordable housing by the end of the month   YES   NO

   _____

   _____

An objective is an intended result of service provision—the nuts and bolts of the plan. Are the following statements objectives?

- Sally will lose two pounds this week. YES   NO

_____

_____

- I will study harder to make an A. YES   NO

_____

_____

- Client will participate in a weekly anger management class for six weeks beginning next week. YES   NO

_____

_____

⬤ Chapter Summary

After the initial assessment phase in the case management process, the case manager and client enter the planning phase. During this time, the case manager and the client work together to review the initial assessment, develop a plan, make use of information systems, and gather additional information. The planning phase begins with a review of the relevant facts gathered during assessment. This includes an examination of information, including the source of the problem, previous attempts at solving the problem, the client's motivations for solving the problem, the client's interests and strengths that may assist problem solving, and barriers that may hinder any attempts to solve the problem. Once this information is gathered, the case manager and the client work together to develop a plan. This process includes setting goals, deciding on objectives, and determining specific interventions.

After the case manager and the client have developed and agreed on the plan, available services are identified. In this phase, the case manager acts much like a broker, identifying service providers and linking service providers and clients together. During this time, case managers may depend on information and referral systems. Part of planning may also include gathering additional information. Case managers frequently rely on interviewing and testing as data collection methods. Interviewing and test administration should be conducted only by professionals who are qualified to do so. Both types of data have potential sources of error, and this should be taken into consideration whenever interpreting results and making decisions with the client.

⬤ Exercise 1: Back to the Future

Planning generally implies future direction; however, in human services it begins with an assessment that looks back rather than forward. The following situation illustrates this reassessment activity:

Frankie and John sought help originally because they desperately needed financial assistance. John, a police officer, was diagnosed with brain cancer about the same time Frankie had their second child, another boy. Shortly after, Frankie's dad died, leaving them his home that he had refinanced to help Frankie and John with their medical expenses. They are now living in the house although they may lose it because John's disability is not enough for them to pay the mortgage. Last Friday evening Frankie discovered they had a winning lottery ticket. Now they have $1.5 million.

Does the probl   to exist? YES   NO

Has it changed

_____

_____

_____

_____

Who is involved at the present time?

_____

_____

_____

_____

Describe any shifts in the environment.

_____

_____

_____

_____

What changes do you anticipate in plan development?

_____

_____

_____

_____

Exercise 2: A Professional's Perspective

Go to the website that accompanies this book: www.thomsonedu.com/counseling/mcclam, Chapter 6, Link 1, to hear Herman Twiggs, a human service professional, talk about his perspective of service plans.

1. Why are service plans important?

_____

_____

_____

2. What criteria should a plan address?

_____

_____

_____

•••••••••••••• Exercise 3: Planning in Your Life

Think for a moment about a trip you've taken recently. You knew your destination but there were also a number of other considerations: Was it a trip you had taken before? Did you know the way or was it a new experience? Did you choose the scenic route or the interstate? Who went with you? When did you plan to arrive at your destination? How many stops did you make? In reality, you do some planning every day—for example, how you will tackle a class assignment, what you will do over the coming weekend, and how you will accomplish everything you've set out to do today. All require planning. Or you may have a larger project ahead of you: losing weight, planning a wedding, finding a job, or moving to another residence. Your assignment here is to select a task or project and develop a plan to guide your actions.

Project: _____

Goal 1:

_____

Objective 1:

_____

_____

_____

Objective 2:

_____

_____

_____

Goal 2:

_____

Objective 1:

_____

_____

_____

Objective 2:

_____

_____

_____

•••••••••••••• Exercise 4: Plan Review

Review the goals and objectives you established in the previous exercise. Evaluate your goals and objectives by responding to the following items:

Goals

Are they broad statements of intent?	YES	NO
Do they specify where I want to be at the end?	YES	NO
Are they reasonable?	YES	NO

Do they reflect my values and preferences?	YES	NO
Are they clear and concise?	YES	NO
Are they achievable?	YES	NO
Objectives		
Does each objective begin with *to* followed by an action verb?	YES	NO
Do my objectives state an intended result?	YES	NO
Does each objective specify *who*, *what*, and *when*?	YES	NO
Do I venture into *why* and *how*?	YES	NO
Is each objective measurable?	YES	NO
Is it attainable?	YES	NO

•••• ● Exercise 5: Working through the Planning Process

1. Read the following case of Renda, a welfare mother.

   I was a client in the human service system for a long time. The beginning of my life as a client actually happened when I was still with my husband. He was not supplying any money to our family. We could not afford diapers, food, or anything for our home. We lived out in the middle of nowhere in a broken-down trailer with no electricity, hot water, things like that. I had to go to Social Services to try to get some food for my child because she literally had no food or diapers. I found out that my husband, now my ex-husband, was using the welfare money to gamble. I finally left my husband due to abuse. I was tired of being beaten up and tired of being emotionally abused by him. At that point, I was totally dependent on the welfare system. I received state funds for taking care of my daughter, medical insurance, and other things. I didn't know where else I could go. I had very few options. I could either go to work at minimum wage or apply for welfare. Applying for welfare would allow me to go back to school, at least for a little while. The social service agencies helped me apply for grants and loans so I could go back to school.

   The very first time I went to a meeting at social services was to gain help not only for my daughter and me, but also for my husband. When I went back the second time to apply for assistance just for my daughter and me, I ended up getting a really wonderful worker, Cindy. When I went in to see her, she could . . . I don't know, we just clicked and it was almost like she said, "You need to cry." And I said, "Yeah." At that point I was living in a women's abuse center. I had no self-esteem, no self-respect. I was in the gutter, literally. I did not know where to go. After my talk with Cindy, she summarized my needs: money, school, insurance, and child care. Of course, she said, that was only her first shot at identifying my problems.

2. Review Renda's statement about her first and second visit with her caseworker and revisit the assessment phase by answering the following questions:

   • How did Renda's problems change?

   _____

   _____

   _____

   _____

   _____

- What do you know about the sources of the problems?

  _____

  _____

  _____

  _____

  _____

- What motivations prompt Renda to solve the problems?

  _____

  _____

  _____

  _____

  _____

- What are Renda's interests and strengths that support the helping process?

  _____

  _____

  _____

  _____

  _____

- What barriers may affect Renda's attempts to resolve the problems?

  _____

  _____

  _____

  _____

  _____

3. Before developing a plan for services, the case manager integrates all information about the client. The planning form that follows Renda's description of her life is one structured way to assemble this information.

   Things were really difficult for me before I left my husband. He broke into my home and further destroyed the trust that I had in people. Here I am, not only abused but I have my home broken into and my daughter is almost kidnapped. So it was really hard. I was as low as any person can get on the earth. Lucky for me, a great family stood behind me. The women at the shelter backed me in everything and sometimes would fight with me to get me to express my feelings. That was one thing that I did not do very well to begin with. I did not openly express how I was feeling or how things were going until the point they would literally have to pull it out of me.

   The shelter is a remodeled old house, and it is beautiful. There was almost a family atmosphere there. When I was at the shelter, three other ladies and their children were there. I had the youngest child. We shared the household chores, like the cooking and the cleaning. We even shared watching each other's children. For example, if I had a court date, I didn't have to worry about child care. I didn't want to drag my one-year-old child to the courthouse. We would do the same when one of the other ladies had to go to court. My daughter and I had one bedroom to ourselves and there was a TV room and a playroom for the kids. And there were four workers. There was one worker who focused on the children who were not able to go to school because they were hiding.

Before I went to the shelter to escape from my husband, I lived in a trailer where I was not able to see anybody because I was scared he would find us. I could not go any place. I was stuck in that trailer, 24 hours a day, 7 days a week. I was never out of that home except for the front porch. So it was very hard for me to get out and see people again.

My daughter also suffered through all of this. She sensed my fear. My husband wanted to kill me and kidnap her. I had a gun. I had double locks on the trailer. I could not let my daughter go outside and play by herself. She was a prisoner in her own home. But I refused to let him have her because I did not want her to grow up in a drug and alcohol environment.

My husband has been in the penitentiary for a while, so she has not seen him. His mother, her grandmother, did take her to the prison once. Now I will not let her see her grandmother either.

My daughter cannot sleep and she has terrible nightmares. She cries for seemingly no reason at all. She did not deserve what she had to go through. I know that she has psychological problems; she will not listen to me. She is very disobedient and sometimes she is violent. I know that her daddy abused her, too. I never saw him do it, but I do know that she had marks on her body. Sometimes I just had to leave her alone with him. We don't really have any concrete evidence, and my daughter will not talk about her father at all.

I told you that I cannot let her out to play by herself. She hates that. Whenever she does go somewhere, she seems to get lost. She just wanders off and does not see any problem with it. In fact, she really does not like anyone telling her what to do. I have had to take her to the emergency room four times this last year because she just pushed physical limits. One day she decided that she would live beneath the sofa. She wasn't really small enough to do this, and she eventually got stuck. I had to cut the bottom of the sofa to get her out, but I didn't get her out safely. The emergency room doctor said that he had heard all kinds of stories, but none like this. She had to have seven stitches in her arm where she cut herself when she tried to wiggle out.

4. Now that you have more information about Renda and her situation, complete the Client Worksheet.

CLIENT WORKSHEET

Client: _____

Date: _____

SOURCE OF INFORMATION
RELEVANT FACTS

CONTRADICTIONS

CLIENT MOTIVATIONS
CLIENT STRENGTHS
CLIENT INTERESTS

5. Assume you are Renda's welfare case manager. List three goals and two objectives for each goal.

Goal 1:

_____

Objective 1:

_____

_____

Objective 2:

_____

_____

Goal 2:

_____

Objective 1:

_____

_____

Objective 2:

_____

_____

Goal 3:

_____

Objective 1:

_____

_____

Objective 2:

_____

_____

6. Evaluate the goals and objectives you have written using the following standards:

Goals

Are they broad statements of intent?	YES	NO
Do they specify where I want to be at the end?	YES	NO
Are they reasonable?	YES	NO
Do they reflect my values and preferences?	YES	NO
Are they clear and concise?	YES	NO
Are they achievable?	YES	NO

Objectives

Does each objective begin with _to_ followed by an action verb?	YES	NO
Do my objectives state an intended result?	YES	NO
Does each objective specify _who_, _what_, and _when_?	YES	NO
Do I venture into _why_ and _how_?	YES	NO
Is each objective measurable?	YES	NO
Is it attainable?	YES	NO

7. Read about the experience Renda and her daughter have with case management.

Cindy was my caseworker for two years. She was the best support for me. Many workers have such large caseloads; they explain the services that you are to receive and then say, "I'll see you again in six months." Cindy was not like that. In fact, she helped me find more services for my daughter and me. She knew a lot of professionals, and they really helped me get what I needed.

During this time I also had some testing. Cindy helped me through this. I had to take a drug and alcohol assessment to determine if I had substance abuse issues. The judge ordered the tests to help decide custody of my daughter. When the welfare office found out about it, they wanted the results. It was really weird. During the testing, they made sure I didn't have any urine on me. They also asked me thousands of questions. And one of the questions that was hardest for me to answer was, "How old were you when you took your first drink?" If I had told them how old I was when I had my first alcoholic drink, they would have said, "Red light! She is an alcoholic." And so I explained, "I am not from the United States. I grew up in Germany. The cultures are different. So when I tell you don't be shocked." They continued to run medical tests. They did blood tests and more urine tests. They had to have four samples, so they would call me up at 7:30 am and ask me to be here at 8:15. I would have to get up and run to the testing office. It was literally random.

I also had to take tests before I could go to college with welfare support. They gave me vocabulary tests and a skills test just to see how well I would do if I went back to college. The highest that you could test was 12th grade 8th month. That is what I tested. I had this test after I had my first interview with Cindy. I think it was like a basic GED test, but I am not positive. I had social studies, English, math, science, a lot of reading. I was put in this room and I had these little bubbles to fill in. They graded it then and there.

Cindy tried to point me in different directions. Each direction meant more interviews, more tests, and more assignments. But I had confidence that she was working for me. She was there with the compassion and caring. At the beginning of service delivery, she put me in touch with agencies that would help supplement my income so I could afford diapers, formula, and other things for my daughter. There were several churches in the county that helped me. One of them was Cindy's church. At one point I was going through a very bad depressive state and the doctor wanted me to take some antidepressants. Medicaid did not cover those. Her church paid, once they had information from the doctor that these were medications that I needed.

Later Cindy helped when my daughter was having trouble. She sent us to a local mental health center, and they did an assessment. They looked at her environment, her physical condition, and her psychological condition. She also was assessed by a genetic center. I had to go through another case manager who took the family tree and the entire family background of both my side of the family as well as my ex-husband's. I had limited knowledge of his family background. Then we went to a screening. They did eye tests on her. They did motor skills tests. They would ask her questions in a certain order. And I also had to answer a questionnaire about her behavior. It came to the point where she was at home hurting herself. She was literally injuring herself. After this screening, they made specific recommendations about where she should go to preschool and the kind of environment she should have. They also said that she was Oppositional Defiant and Attention Deficit Disorder.

8. Prior to service delivery, the case manager may need additional information about the client. Interviews and tests are two ways of gathering this additional information. Renda describes some of her experiences with interviews and tests.

- If you were the case manager how would you use this information?

    _____

    _____

    _____

    _____

- List the interviews and tests that Renda describes and summarize their purposes.

    _____

    _____

    _____

    _____

- Add the information gained from these tests to fill in the Client Worksheet (4). How does this information change your goals and objectives? Be specific.

_____

_____

_____

_____

_____

•••••••••••••••• ● Exercise 6: Test Resources

A new agency policy requires that all individuals accepted for services complete an interest inventory. Your supervisor has asked that you select three different inventories to present to the staff for their consideration.

1. Review the information on testing in Chapter 6 of *Generalist Case Management*.

2. Identify sources of information about testing. List three.

_____

_____

_____

3. What information do you expect to get from each source?

Source 1:

_____

_____

_____

Source 2:

_____

_____

_____

Source 3:

_____

_____

_____

•••••••••••••• ● Exercise 7: Test Analysis

Your agency has decided to use the Mooney Problem Checklist as an initial interviewing and counseling tool. You have been asked to present an analysis of this instrument in the next staff meeting. To do that, you must find the following information:

1. Title and any abbreviations or acronyms

_____

2. Author and institution or affiliation

_____

3. Publisher

_____

4. Copyright date

_____

5. Purpose and recommended use

_____

_____

_____

6. Dimensions, subtests, or content areas. Describe each briefly.

_____

_____

_____

_____

_____

7. Administration. Describe briefly. Include timing and instructions.

_____

_____

_____

_____

_____

_____

8. Describe scoring procedures. How are scores expressed?

_____

_____

9. What information is provided about validity? How is validity demonstrated? Is this test correlated with other tests? Any external criteria?

_____

_____

_____

_____

10. What is the reliability and how was it determined?

_____

_____

_____

_____

11. Are norms tables provided? Describe.

_____

_____

_____

_____

12. Is a test profile provided?

_____

_____

_____

_____

13. How will you explain the scores to your client?

_____

_____

_____

_____

14. List your sources of information.

_____

_____

_____

_____

15. What other sources of information would be helpful?

_____

_____

_____

_____

●·············· In More Depth: It's "Our" Plan!

Planning comes naturally to many of us. For some, the process occurs in our heads. We never write a thing—it's strictly a mental activity. Others depend on writing, usually in the form of lists. These identify the tasks to be accomplished, the items needed, or both. Helping agencies and organizations require formal plans, documents that capture the planning process in writing. In this age of accountability and client involvement, plans also require the client's signature—evidence that the client is aware of the plan and is in agreement with the goals, objectives, and activities. A key to the success of plan development and the resulting signed document is a collaborative relationship with the client.

Successful case management requires client involvement throughout the process, but one of its most critical places is in plan development. This activity is similar to the trip planning activity in Exercise 3. On the trip to a written plan, you now have a passenger and the efforts of both the driver and the passenger are necessary to arrive at the destination. If you and your client are going in different directions, then you both have a problem. An efficient trip will have a single destination, two drivers who share the duty, some stops along the way, and an agreement about the route. Upon reaching the destination, both travelers are satisfied. The same applies to plan development. The goal is a written document that pleases both the client and the case manager. At different points in plan development, the case manager and client may alternate taking the lead. Sometimes it's not a smooth process; for example, there are bumps in the road, other passengers join them, roadblocks appear, or alternate routes are necessary. A collaborative effort enables arrival at a destination (or written document in case management language) that satisfies all involved. This section focuses on the skills that are necessary to make this collaboration succeed.

One approach to client involvement is the case manager's familiarity with the plan used by the employing agency or organization. Many agencies use a form that is completed by filling in the blanks. Other agencies require a plan that involves composing prose—a written proposal for services. Others may have a fairly elementary chart. Examples of different planning documents follow. As you examine these documents, identify the components common to all of them. Knowing what the plan requires for completion will help you use your skills to encourage client involvement in making decisions about the plan's content.

Example 1

THE PLAN

CLIENT:_____ Age:_____

PROBLEM:_____

Goal 1:

_____

Objective:

_____

_____

By (date): _____ Responsible Person:_____

Objective:

_____

_____

By (date): _____Responsible Person:_____

Goal 2:

_____

Objective:

_____

_____

By (date):_____Responsible Person:_____

Objective:

_____

_____

By (date):_____Responsible Person:_____

Goal 3:

_____

Objective:

_____

_____

By (date):_____Responsible Person:_____

Objective:

_____

_____

By (date):_____Responsible Person:_____

Example 2

Excerpt from a high school Individualized Education Plan with transition goals for a student with a severe disability.

Student: Bob Robbins	Meeting Place: _____ 00/00/00 _____
	Graduation : _____ XX/XX/XX _____

Participants:

Parent(s): Mrs. Robbins _____

School: William Bailey, Special Education Teacher _____

DHS Case Manager: Susan Love, Developmental Disabilities Agency _____

DVR Case Manager: N/A _____

Planning Area: Vocational Services	Responsible Person	Timelines
Transition Goal:		
Bob will initiate work training Progress in Wasatch Work Crew Program	Mr. Bailey	4/15/XX
Objectives/Activities		
1. To complete application process	Ms. Robbins Ms. Love	3/1/XX
2. To buy city bus pass	Ms. Robbins	3/1/ XX
3. To teach bus route to Wasatch business office	Mr. Bailey	3/15/XX
4. To set up planning meeting with Wasatch WCP director	Ms. Love	4/30/XX

Example 3

Date Completed:

Consumer Name:

Case Manager:

Life Domain:

❏ Financial   ❏ Alcohol & Drug

❏ Physical   ❏ Vocation / Educational

❏ Social Support   ❏ Leisure / Recreational

❏ Living Arrangement

If this domain has been addressed in a previous service plan, document outcomes/progress of that plan here, and proceed to plan below.

❏   This domain has not been previously addressed—proceed to plan below.

PLAN	Responsible Party	Target Dates	Outcomes
Long-Term Goal:			
Measurable Objectives:			

_____   _____
Consumer Signature   Date   Case Manager Signature   Date

Consumer signature is indication of consumer involvement and understanding of the plan.

___   Participated, Refused To Sign
___   Refused To Participate
___   Unable To Participate   Why Not? _____

_____
Supervisor Signature   Date

_____
Family/Significant Other Signature (if applicable)   Date

As you examined these documents, you probably noted that common to all of them are three components: goals and objectives, activities to reach them, and in one of them, a place for the signatures of the client and the case manager. The signatures at the end of the plan are an indication of the partnership that was integral to its development. What are the skills necessary to make this happen? How do the case manager and the client become partners in plan development? The following activities provide a foundation for the partnership.

Information

The client has the right to know what the planning process is and may have questions about it. What is the plan? What does it look like? Why is a signature necessary? Is it carved in stone? Do I have to do everything? Who else will know about it? What if I fail? How do we fill it in? Demystifying the planning process is an important beginning. It is much easier to participate in an activity if you know what it is and what the expectations are for your participation.

Before explaining the process, the case manager carefully considers the level of explanation and uses words that the client will understand. Depending on how much information the client can grasp at one time, the case manager also asks for questions ("Do you have any questions about the form?"), provides clarification ("Goal is a complicated term. Maybe it would help if I gave you some examples."), focuses on strengths ("I remember when you told me about building a birdhouse and being able to follow the plan. This is a similar process, only you and I will come up with the plan!"), and requests feedback ("Tell me what you think about all this."). Finally, the case manager listens carefully to the client's comments and suggestions. This particular moment in plan development can be a significant and positive step for the client. Focusing on a new beginning, grasping the steps in the process, and having a say in his or her own service plan are empowering.

Part of sharing information involves "nuts and bolts." Often case managers skip this part, assuming that the client knows or that the client will "catch on." Many times clients don't know who will do what when, how they will know when they reach the end, what their role is, what the case manager does, and how long the whole process will take. Role induction, a term Meier and Davis (2005) use, describes the client's introduction to the process and what the expectations are for his or her involvement. Understanding these facets adds structure to the process and clearly spells out the client's role and the case manager's role. It would be a mistake to skip this step if client participation is important.

Client Input

It is within the case manager's power to make the client a partner in the process. The case of Frankie and John in Exercise 1 illustrates the importance of reassessment. Before the case manager and the client can move forward, they must step back. Has the client changed? Does the problem still exist? Any shifts in the environment? In Frankie and John's situation, drastic changes required a change in the service plan. So this "look back" is important. A primary source of information in this activity is the client. This marks the beginning of client involvement in planning.

Client input is also important throughout the rest of planning. A number of examples illustrate this involvement. As the client and the case manager move forward to establish goals and objectives, the client's values and preferences are considered. The evaluation of the goals as realistic and attainable and the sequencing of steps is also a joint effort.

The case manager also continues to focus on client strengths. Finally, the client is charged with the responsibility for providing updates on progress, changes, or problems.

None of this may come naturally to a client. In fact, it may represent an entirely new way of thinking and call for new skills. In the past, clients may have been limited to convergent thinking—that is, believing that there is only one answer or solution to a problem. Probes and reinforcing statements are ways to encourage a divergent approach—if several right answers or solutions are possible. Examples of probes and reinforcing statements follow.

Probes that seek more information from the client

- ◆ What would your life be like if . . .
- ◆ List some changes that make sense to you.

- ✦ What would you be doing differently with other people?
- ✦ How would your behavior be different from the way it is now?

<u>Reinforcing statements to support and encourage the client's participation</u>

- ✦ That's an interesting idea.
- ✦ These ideas are really creative.
- ✦ Good thinking! Any more ideas?

Relationship Development

Planning development offers many opportunities to continue to build and strengthen the relationship between the case manager and the client. Numerous skills contribute to communicating to the client that the case manager understands the client's thoughts and feelings (Brammer & MacDonald, 2003). These include listening (eye contact, nodding, verbal following), clarifying ("Let's talk about what's going on with you"), perception checking ("You seemed confused about these two goals. Is that right?"), paraphrasing (a brief restatement of the client's words). Of these, listening is the key. In fact, effectiveness as a helper is tied to the case manager's ability to communicate to the client that the case manager understands the client's thoughts, feelings, and behaviors. From this understanding comes confidence in the case manager's ability to help.

Other helping skills that facilitate relationship development are reflecting, supporting, and summarizing. Read the following dialogue to see how these responses facilitate both understanding and the relationship.

Client: I was so angry after I talked with the woman who answered the phone. She was no help at all, and I didn't know where else to turn. And she didn't help with that either. I was abandoned.

Helper: At a time when you really needed some direction, you didn't get it and you are still furious about your conversation with her. (Reflecting)

Client: Exactly. I don't think she should be doing that job if she's not going to be helpful to people who call. I was desperate. I didn't know where to turn. We had nothing—no food, no home, no transportation, no money. It is devastating to lose everything. A fire destroys everything. Our lives are gone.

Helper: As awful as this has been for you and your family, and it has been a terrible experience, you have a safe place to stay for a month or so. That was very resourceful of you. And now you have time to think about what you want to do. (Supporting).

Client: Yes, we have some time to think about the future—a place to live, going back to work, school. In a way, starting over is okay. It's just so hard to lose things you can't replace. Those are the real losses.

Helper: Yes, they are, and you must be sad when you think about the pictures and other family mementos that are gone. It's another loss to cope with. We've talked about a number of these losses today. Let's take a minute and look back at what we've discussed. You've been through a terrible time, and we've talked about the losses you've experienced as well as the frustrations that you've experienced in getting help. How does it look to you at this point? (Summarizing)

During plan development there will be times when the client will ask for information: "Where should I go to see about this?" or "What happens during a psychological evaluation?" or "Who can tell me about that?" Many times it is appropriate to respond to the client's request for information. Other times the client asks for advice ("What should I do about this?" "What do you think I should say to her?" "Tell me how to respond to that."), And here the case manager should exercise caution. Limitations to advice are that clients usually don't follow it or, if they follow it, they may find it is invalid and end up blaming the case manager for things not turning out right. A more effective approach to informing is being tentative ("One approach might be . . ."), being sure of your knowledge or expertise, and knowing the sources of your information (Brammer & MacDonald, 2003). Nothing will destroy the relationship faster than invalid advice, bad information, or coercion.

Although the case manager has used the planning process and is an expert in reassessment, writing a service plan, and gathering additional information, it is important to pace the work to fit the client's needs and skills. The client may need additional time reassessing his or her situation or may not be clear about priorities or goals. Respecting the client's needs for more time conveys that the process is for the client and the planning is a collaboration.

Success

The final product of plan development is the written plan. This document will demonstrate the client's involvement in the process and the partnership between the client and the case manager. It will take the form of the assignment or designation of roles and responsibilities, reflect the values and preferences of the client, and adhere to the rules and regulations of the agency. Finally, the signatures of the client and the case manager will be the final evidence that it is "our plan."

Case Study   Gloria came to the United States from Puerto Rico to study sign language and interpreting. There are very few people in Puerto Rico with these skills. Her husband is disabled, his disability check is not enough to support a family of five, and she wants training so that she can help support her family.

From her pastor in Puerto Rico, she learns about a training program at a university in the southeastern United States. In addition, the program pays each participant a stipend for living expenses as well as tuition and fees. Gloria moves to the United States and begins the program. Her husband and three children eventually join her, and they move to a two-bedroom apartment in the university housing complex. In addition to crowded living conditions, neither the husband nor the children speak English. Her husband never leaves the apartment. They are settled one month when the problems begin. Additional information about Gloria's history, her family, and her decision to pursue education and training in the United States appears in *Introduction to Human Services: Cases and Applications* (Chapter 7).

•••••••••••• Exercise 8: Meet Gloria

 Your assignment is to meet Gloria and learn about her problems. First, view the introductory comments from Gloria on the website that accompanies this book, Chapter 6, Link 2, and respond to the following questions:

1. What are your initial impressions of Gloria?

_____

_____

_____

_____

2. Describe all of the times you have difficulty understanding her.

_____

_____

_____

_____

3. What do you know about Puerto Rico and its culture?

_____

_____

_____

_____

_____

Exercise 9: Problem Statements

Gloria briefly describes each problem she encountered after one month with her family in the United States. Write problem statements based on what she says.

Problem One
Problem Statement:

_____

_____

Problem Two
Problem Statement:

_____

_____

Problem Three
Problem Statement:

_____

_____

Problem Four
Problem Statement:

_____

_____

Problem Five
Problem Statement:

_____

_____

Problem Six
Problem Statement:

_____

_____

Exercise 10: Developing a Plan of Services

You now have a sense of the experiences Gloria has had and some of the challenges she faces. Develop a plan of services to assist Gloria. Rather than providing services for each problem, review your problem statements and initial goals. Think about ways to combine the needs she has to most efficiently and effectively plan.

Case Manager's Name:	Date:	Consumer's Name:	Case Number:

Planned Frequency of Contact:

Life Domain (check one) ____ **Living Arrangements** ____ **Vocational/Educational**

____ **Social Support**   ____ **Financial**   ____ **Health**

____ **Leisure/Recreational**

Long Term Goal:

Short-Term Goals and Action Steps	Responsibility for C/CM	Date to be Accomplished	Date Accomplished	Comments

_____   _____
Case Manager's Signature   Date   Consumer's Signature   Date

_____   _____
Supervisor Signature   Date   Other Signature & Title   Date

_____ Consumer Participated in Personal Plan   _____ Consumer Refused to Participate in Personal Plan Process, but Refused to Sign

·············● # Exercise 11: Anticipated Challenges

You have listened to Gloria, identified her problems, and developed a service plan for her. Answer the following questions.

1. Identify the challenges you think YOU might face in working with Gloria, who has a different cultural background from you. Specifically, how are the following illustrated with this client?

   Accent:

   _____

   _____

   _____

   Language:

   _____

   _____

   _____

   Cultural norms:

   _____

   _____

   _____

   Gender issues:

   _____

   _____

   _____

   Collectivist culture:

   _____

   _____

   _____

2. As you work with Gloria, how will you encourage her participation in plan development?

   _____

   _____

   _____

3. Describe her values and preferences based on her discussion of the six problems listed in Item 1 of this Exercise.

   _____

   _____

   _____

4. What skills would you use to encourage her to share values, preferences, and other information about herself and her situation? Provide examples.

_____

_____

_____

5. How can the plan reflect her values and preferences? Are there goals and objectives that you would change now that you better understand her values and preferences?

_____

_____

_____

6. Do you think she will sign the plan you developed? Why or why not?

_____

_____

Self-Assessment

1. Describe three important concepts related to service delivery planning.

_____

_____

_____

_____

2. Explain how these concepts support your service planning work with Gloria.

_____

_____

_____

_____

3. Review the planning forms presented in this chapter. Which form seems most useful for you to use in planning? Why?

_____

_____

_____

_____

 ## Pretest Answers

1. Need to know if problem has changed, same client resources available, any shift in agency priorities (p. 133).
2. Generally goals, plans and objectives (p. 138). Otherwise, eligibility, program objectives, intermediate objectives, services, methods of checking progress, client and agency responsibilities, client's view of program, and signatures (pp. 134, 136–137).
3. Identify all agencies and available services, input them into a directory that you continuously update through networking and other methods (p. 145). Then identify and prioritize client problems, and match them to the services available with attention to client values and concerns.
4. Interviewing has sources of error (halo effect and general standoutishness) and limited reliability but with more structure can have less error (pp. 146–147). Testing may be used to complement interviews and serves to verify information gathered from an interview, but one must understand the test: its purpose, development, reliability and validity, administration and scoring, procedures, as well as characteristics of norm groups and limits and strengths of the test (p. 149).
5. No for those too broad and not stated in achievable terms; yes for clear and specific with a timeline; yes states one specific result that is realistic and measurable with a target date; no, no specific or measurable action and no target date; yes, specific and achievable and measurable action with a target date (pp. 138–139).

References

Brammer, L., & MacDonald, G. (2003). *The helping relationship: Process and skills* (8th ed.). Needham Heights, MA: Allyn and Bacon.

Meier, S. T., & Davis, S. (2005). *The elements of counseling*. Pacific Grove, CA: Brooks/Cole/Thomson.

Building a Case File

Building a case file is the subject of Chapter 7 in *Generalist Case Management*. This chapter identifies and examines the types of information that are part of the client's case file. They include medical, psychological, social, educational, and vocational information. The following exercises enable you to practice your skills in building a case file.

 Pretest

After reading Chapter 7 in *Generalist Case Management*, answer the following questions and complete the items.

1. How does medical information contribute to your knowledge of a client?

_____

_____

_____

2. Identify the four elements of medical terminology and apply them to the medical term "hypothermia."

_____

_____

_____

_____

3. What are some strategies you can use to obtain a good psychological evaluation?

_____

_____

_____

4. What are the advantages and limitations of a social history?

_____

_____

_____

5. Discuss the client's role in building the case file.

_____

_____

_____

_____

Chapter Summary

When working with clients, case managers build case files that include information related to the agency's goals and the individual client's needs. A case file often includes medical, psychological, social, educational, and vocational information. Accurate and up-to-date medical information is a crucial part of the case file, especially for clients with medical issues or disabilities. Sometimes this information helps determine eligibility for services and determines the client's functional limitations or potential for rehabilitation. The case manager needs to be familiar with medical terminology in medical exams and diagnostic reports. Psychological reports are also important documents in the client's case file. The objectives of a psychological evaluation are to contribute to the understanding of the individual client and to provide justification for particular services. Case managers should also be familiar with language and terminology used in psychological evaluations.

The client's past history and present situation help the case manager understand the client's problem-solving strategies, his or her developmental stages, and the nature of interpersonal relationships. Taking a social history provides the case manager with information and helps build the relationship between the client and the case manager. Gaps in information can also be addressed. Depending on the type of services the agency provides and the needs of the client, other types of information may also be included in the client's case file. Educational information, such as test scores, classroom behavior, and attendance records may be relevant in some cases. Also, for many clients, vocational information, such as employment history and work habits, may be relevant, depending on the needs of the client and the services he or she will receive.

Exercise 1: Using Other Professionals

Gathering additional information about a client often involves consulting with other professionals, requesting evaluations or reports from them, or both. Who are these other professionals?

1. List four professionals from whom you might seek additional client information. What credentials would you expect them to have?

_____

_____

_____

_____

2. Describe the information that you think each could provide about a client.

_____

_____

_____

_____

_____

_____

3. An important first step in seeking additional information is to have the client's permission to do so. How would you explain the need to gather additional information to the client?

_____

_____

_____

_____

Exercise 2: What Information to Gather?

One of the first steps in gathering information is to decide what to do. This process begins with identifying the problem and deciding what information will help you complete a picture of the client.

1. Read about Janis.

Janis Jones has just come to live with her grandmother in a small house in a community near the university. She is 12 years old and runs with a "rough" crowd as her grandmother describes it. She and her mother never really bonded, but her mother retains legal custody so that she can cover Janis with her insurance. Janis talks back to her grandmother, disobeys her, and pays little attention to the rules. About two months ago, she screamed at her grandmother in the parking lot of a movie theater and was hysterical for two hours. Her mother and her grandmother believe she needs to see a counselor and she has agreed. The counselor thinks she is depressed and refers her to a physician for medication. Unfortunately, her behavior is getting out of control. She's becoming more and more defiant, staying out late, and not telling her grandmother where she is going. Her grandmother thinks she may be experimenting with drugs. Yesterday Janis slapped her grandmother and threatened to kill her.

2. Identify the presenting problem in this case.

_____

_____

_____

_____

3. What other possible problems do you suspect?

_____

_____

_____

_____

4. What questions do you have about Janis and her situation?

_____

_____

_____

_____

_____

5. What information would you like to add to her case file so that you have a more complete picture of this client?

_____

_____

_____

_____

_____

6. If you decide to refer Janis to other professionals to gather additional information, identify the professionals, state the purpose of the referral, and write the specific questions you would like answered.

Professional 1: _____

Purpose: _____

_____

_____

Questions: _____

_____

_____

_____

Professional 2: _____

_____

Purpose: _____

_____

_____

Questions: _____

_____

_____

_____

Professional 3: _____

Purpose: _____

_____

_____

Questions: _____

_____

_____

_____

_____

● Exercise 3: Gathering Information and the Service Plan

Often, gathering additional information is part of the service plan because it may require the expenditure of agency funds.

1. Review what you have learned about writing service plans and the information you need to have a more complete picture of Janis.
2. Develop a service plan for Janis.

Client: Janis Jones

Goal: To gather additional information to complete the case file

Objective 1: _____

_____

By (date): _____ Responsible Person: _____

Objective 2: _____

_____

By (date): _____ Responsible Person: _____

Objective 3: _____

_____

By (date): _____ Responsible Person: _____

In More Depth: The Problems of Mental Illness

Mental illness is a serious challenge facing the United States in the 21st century. Although it is difficult to know the exact number of individuals who experience mental illness in any given span of time, the National Institute of Mental Health (1998) projected that approximately 22.1 percent of American adults, or 60.1 million people, experience mental illness in a given year. The individual, social, and economic costs are considerable.

Because of the pervasiveness of mental illness in the United States, most case managers will encounter individuals who have been diagnosed as mentally ill or who meet the criteria for diagnosis. Examples of four of these situations follow: (1) the case manager is actually working with the persistently mentally ill; (2) the case manager is working with a client who has not previously been diagnosed but the case manager suspects the client meets the criteria for diagnosis; (3) the case manager has a client who has been diagnosed with a mental illness in the past; (4) the case manager is working with a client and one or more members of the client's family are mentally ill. The information in this section helps case managers in the latter three categories; case managers working with the persistently mentally ill require knowledge, skills, and values about mental illness beyond the scope of this chapter. Learning about how mental illness is defined in the United States, examining the theories of mental illness that predict client behavior and guide treatment, and understanding the variability of diagnosis help the case manager interact with clients and their families. This information also helps case managers understand information in client files that relates to mental health.

Defining Mental Illness

Professional criteria used to define mental illness, found in the current *Diagnostic and Statistical Manual of Mental Disorders, Fourth Edition, Text Revision (DSM-IV-TR)*, represent a way for professionals to distinguish between normal and abnormal behavior. This edition of the manual, written and published by the American Psychiatric Association, establishes criteria useful for determining diagnoses of mental illness. Professionals use three criteria to determine mental illness (Spitzer & Wilson, 1975). First, mental illness is a psychological disorder or condition responsible for changing an individual's behavior and physical functioning. Second, mental illness is a disorder that, at its worst, causes stress, impairs social functioning, and/or causes the individual to wish to alter his or her current condition. Third, the mental illness is distinct from other medical conditions and responds to treatment.

In our culture, mental illness is defined as a disorder within an individual that results in a deviance from standards of behavior that society views as normal. Social norms indicate how members of society assume others will behave. Some behaviors, seen as disordered thinking or aberrant behavior, become classified as deviant. Examples of these behaviors include continually beginning fights, drinking or abusing drugs to excess, staying in bed all day and all night, and hearing voices or seeing apparitions, to name a few. Definitions of aberrant behavior are not static or constant. Because the norms related to defining mental illness continually change, the definitions of mental illnesses change as well (Morrison, 1995). For example, homosexuality, defined in earlier editions of the *DSM*, was a diagnosable mental illness. Today, by current definitions in the latest edition, the *DSM-IV-TR*, it is not. The changes to be published in the *DSM-V* in 2010, will reflect the research in the early years of the 21st century. Responding to the criticism that there is little recognition for the effects of race, ethnicity, and culture (Neighbors, Trierweiler, & Muroff, 2003), the next edition will reflect new findings such as how racism can be integrated into the diagnostic criteria (Cockerham, 2006).

Criticism of the *DSM* focuses on the accuracy of its diagnosis, specifically concerning the intensity or number of criteria required for a specific diagnosis (Horwitz, 2002). For example, to be diagnosed with a Major Depressive Disorder, an individual must have five symptoms. The individuals must experience a depressed mood for at least two weeks and have at least four other symptoms, such as significant weight loss or gain, fatigue or loss of energy nearly every day, diminished ability to think or concentrate, and recurrent thoughts of death, to name a few (Fauman, 2002). What if the individual has the four other symptoms, but the depression only lasts for 10 days? The individual finds relief for a few days and then the depression begins again. There would be some disagreement among clinicians whether the individual could be diagnosed with a depressive disorder (Sorenson, Mors, & Thomsen, 2005).

Theories of Mental Illnesses

One purpose of theories of mental illness is to help provide a framework for understanding the nature of mental illness. Within a theoretical framework, professionals are able to explain causes and symptoms, propose treatments, and predict successes of and barriers to treatment. The following five models approach mental illness differently, each providing different perspectives about the causes and possible cures (Cockerham, 2006).

Medical Model

Within the framework of the medical model, mental illness is seen as a disease or is considered disease-like, and the illness is treated using medical approaches. The professional attributes the abnormalities to physiological, biochemical, or genetic causes. The procedures or treatments focus on medical procedures such as psychopharmacology, electroshock therapy, and psychosurgery. Physicians try to uncover the cause of the mental disorder and subsequently treat it. For many individuals with mental illness, psychopharmacology allows them to lead fairly normal lives, but this intervention is not a cure. Limitations of this model include a lack of consideration of the social context and little attention to personal problems (Cockerham, 2006).

Psychoanalytic Model

The focus on internal factors that contribute to mental health and mental illness characterizes this model. Abnormal behavior is viewed in psychological terms; instinctual forces drive the individual, who is either unable to control them or is unaware of them. According to the tenets of the psychoanalytic model, mental illnesses exhibit themselves in four ways. First, the illness expresses itself as a personality disorder, suggesting the individual acts out internal conflicts in the external world. Second, an individual expresses illness as neuroses, better known as anxiety and depressive disorders, and lacks coping skills to deal with problems in living. Third, there is a set of illnesses resulting in physical illness whose cause is attributed to stress and tension. This mental illness is considered a psychosocial disorder. The fourth expression of mental illness is psychotic: The sense of self or the ego disintegrates, resulting in a loss of ability to cope with reality. Treatments or interventions include long-term therapy to reduce or eliminate the emotional problems originating in the past that underlie these mental illnesses. Short-term therapy begins with the present problems or conflicts and seeks to uncover unfounded assumptions through interviews and discussion (Cockerham, 2006).

Social Learning Model

Learning theories and techniques of behavioral conditioning provide the foundation for this model. The underlying belief is that behaviors are learned and they can be unlearned and replaced with more socially appropriate behaviors. The treatment focuses on behaviors that can be observed and measured. Treatments include desensitization, positive reinforcement, aversive conditioning or punishment, and contingency contracting. The limitations of the social learning model focus on the efficacy of the treatment. Can multiple problems be solved with simple behavior changes? How long do behavior changes last after treatment? Can behaviors in one setting be generalized to another setting (Cockerham, 2006)?

Social Stress Model

This model suggests that individuals experience multiple stressors throughout their lives. Difficulties occur when the individual's usual coping strategies fail, and the stress continues and heightens. This model recognizes that stress is partially a subjective response to situations; individuals respond very differently to the same stressors. Sources of stress include environmental demands such as loss of employment, accidents, and high-density living. Personality characteristics also contribute to limited or failed coping skills.

Individuals may also have a genetic predisposition to mental illness, and stressful situations trigger biochemical reactions resulting in abnormal behavior. Mental illnesses such as post-traumatic stress disorder (PTSD) increase an individual's fear and anxiety, actually causing physical changes in the body. Over time, this can result in physical illness such as heart disease, headaches, and ulcers. Treatments include an increase in social support, cognitive behavioral therapy that focuses on the subjective perception of stress, and improvement of coping skills by teaching about the importance of exercise and meditation and helping individuals develop strong social relationships. This model is relatively new and research that supports the theory continues (Cockerham, 2006).

Antipsychiatric Model

From this model emerges a rejection of the term or concept of mental illness or mental disorder. Rather, behavior results from problems in living and conflicting social values. Behavior traditionally viewed as deviant is simply behavior that does not fit within culturally determined norms. Thomas Szasz (1987) makes the case that mental illness is not sickness. He claims that there is no physical disease, the criteria for determining mental illness are subjective, not objective, and the criteria represent social, not medical, norms. Although this model does not represent particular treatments or interventions, it does suggest a different way of viewing mental illness (Cockerham, 2006).

Variability of Diagnosis

As we discussed earlier, case managers often encounter case files that contain one or more diagnoses of mental illnesses. Sometimes a case file has detailed information about the diagnosis, including specific criteria used to make the diagnosis and extensive information about the clients' demeanor and behavior. Other times there is only a *DSM-IV-TR* diagnosis such as Generalized Anxiety Disorder, Sexual and Gender Identity Disorders, or Substance Abuse. Many clients have a history of diagnoses, and often these diagnoses change over time. Regardless of how the diagnosis is presented in the case file, there are limitations to the diagnostic procedure. Understanding these limitations helps the case manager evaluate materials in the client's file and think about a client's mental health status.

Clinical judgment plays an important part in the assessment of mental illnesses. Clinicians differ in their training, years of experience, and experience with specific populations. Clinicians also gather information in different ways, including interviewing, using standardized tests or free association, asking different types of questions, and relying on client reports or reports from family and friends. They may gather information over a series of weeks rather than one or two consecutive sessions. They also differ in what they observe about the client's behavior and how they interpret information. All of this influences the decisions clinicians make and the conclusions they draw about a client's symptoms and diagnosis (Fauman, 2002; Hartman, 1998; Whitley, 2005). For example, an AIDS patient may present symptoms of depression such as self-reporting a depressed mood almost every day, indicating that there is nothing in his or her life that is enjoyable, and feeling a lack of energy every day. One clinician might see the depressive symptoms as a result of having AIDS. Another clinician may view the depression as a mental disorder exacerbated by having AIDS (Walker & Spengler, 1995).

Individuals with the same disorder can present symptoms in a variety of ways (Fauman, 2002). Described next is an example where individuals have been diagnosed with attention deficit hyperactivity disorder (ADHD), but they meet the criteria for the disorder in different ways. The following explanation of the variation of ADHD describes the ways the disorder may present (National Institute of Mental Health, 2003).

Symptoms of ADHD

The principal characteristics of ADHD are *inattention*, *hyperactivity*, and *impulsivity*. These symptoms appear early in a child's life. Because many normal children may have these symptoms, but at a low level, or the symptoms may be caused by another disorder, it is important that the child receive a thorough examination and appropriate diagnosis by a well-qualified professional.

Symptoms of ADHD will appear over the course of many months, often with the symptoms of impulsiveness and hyperactivity preceding those of inattention, which may not emerge for a year or more. Different symptoms may appear in different settings, depending on the demands the situation may pose for the child's self-control. A child who "can't sit still" or is otherwise disruptive will be noticeable in school, but the inattentive daydreamer may be overlooked. The impulsive child who acts before thinking may be considered just a "discipline problem," while the child who is passive or sluggish may be viewed as merely unmotivated. Yet both may have different types of ADHD. All children are sometimes restless, sometimes act without thinking, sometimes daydream the time away. When the child's hyperactivity, distractibility, poor concentration, or impulsivity begin to affect performance in school, social relationships with other children, or behavior at home, ADHD may be suspected. But because the symptoms vary so much across settings, ADHD is not easy to diagnose. This is especially true when inattentiveness is the primary symptom.

According to the most recent version of the *Diagnostic and Statistical Manual of Mental Disorders*[2] (*DSM-IV-TR*), there are three patterns of behavior that indicate ADHD. People with ADHD may show several signs of being consistently inattentive. They may have a pattern of being hyperactive and impulsive far more than others of their age. Or they may show all three types of behavior. This means that there are three subtypes of ADHD recognized by professionals. These are the *predominantly hyperactive-impulsive type* (that does not show significant inattention); the *predominantly inattentive type* (that does not show significant hyperactive-impulsive behavior) sometimes called ADD—an outdated term for this entire disorder; and the *combined type* (that displays both inattentive and hyperactive-impulsive symptoms) [NIMH, 2003].

The information about mental illness presented in the *DSM-IV-TR* helps case managers read the case files of clients more cautiously. Below are several exercises that will allow you to consider information about client mental health and ask questions and draw conclusions.

··············•··· Exercise 4: The Mental Health of a Client

A 15-year-old client is currently in residence at your locked facility, She has been at the facility for two weeks and has been assigned to you for case management. This means that you work with professionals within the residential facility, professionals outside the facility, and her family. You are chairing a staffing for her in two days where various professionals will meet to talk about her situation. You know from talking with other staff that there is a real concern about her diagnosis. The diagnosis will guide treatment goals and receipt of insurance funds to cover her stay at your facility. She has been receiving treatment since she was five years of age.

To prepare for the staffing, you decide to re-read her files, focusing on information in them that describe any mental health issues. Table 7.1 presents your notes.

After reading the information about the 15-year-old client, answer the following information about what you know about her current mental status and her history.

1. What is your over all impression of this client's mental status?

_____

_____

_____

_____

2. Describe the different diagnoses that she has received during the past 10 years and categorize each according to one of the five models of mental disorder described in the "In More Depth" section. Provide a rationale for your choice of models for each diagnosis.

DIAGNOSIS	MODEL	RATIONALE

TABLE 7-1 ◆ NOTES ON MENTAL HEALTH OF FEMALE CLIENT AGE 15

Year	Age of Client	Facility	Professional	Diagnosis	Treatment
1996	5	Child and Family	Social Worker	Behavior is aggressive and out of control – no details	Behavioral Intervention
1997	6	Child and Family	Psychologist	Behavioral problems, hitting parents and brother. Spit at teacher at school. Cussed other children.	School counseling. Group counseling for anger management.
1998	7	Department of Human Services	Referred for suspected child abuse. Psychologist	Assessment is Conduct Disorder – no details.	Referred to Child and Family Services for Counseling and for Family Counseling. Placed in Foster Care for 1 week and then returned to parents.
2001	10	Psychiatric Outpatient Clinic	Referred by school; inability to work in school; aggressive behavior	Assessment by Clinic Diagnosis – ADHD – no details.	Resident of Clinic for 2 weeks; medications. Behavioral interventions. Social skills training.
2002	11	Mobile Crisis Unit In-Patient Psychiatric Clinic	Attempted suicide with aspirin and antihistamines.	Assessment by Clinic – Substance Abuse.	10-day stay – no details.
2006	15	Juvenile Court	Shoplifting; Abusing store clerk when confronted.	Assessment by Social Worker appointed by the court. Diagnosis – Substance Abuse – no details.	Residential Treatment Center – 3 months.
2006	15	Juvenile Court	Shoplifting; Hitting and biting arresting officer. Referred to Department of Human Services Psychological Assessment	Psychological Assessment – Bipolar Intake Interview – uncommunicative, low self-esteem, compliant, perhaps eating disorder	Residential Treatment – Current Medications for Depression and Psychotic Symptoms.

3. Explain why you believe that this client, with over 10 years of treatment, has been diagnosed with so many mental disorders.

_____

_____

_____

_____

4. Use a favorite search engine to locate the National Institute of Mental Health (NIMH) website. Find descriptions of each of the illnesses described in the case and provide a definition for each of them.

_____

_____

_____

_____

_____

_____

5. Given what you understand about this client's mental health history, what recommendations for assessment and treatment will you give at the staffing?

_____

_____

_____

_____

•••••••••••••• Exercise 5: Mental Health Assessment

1. Go to the website that accompanies this book: www.thomsonedu.com/counseling/mcclam, Chapter 7, Link 1, and read the following case of Charles Clark prepared by a local mental health professional. Then complete the following items and answer the questions about this report.
2. Provide a summary of your impressions of this report.

_____

_____

_____

_____

_____

_____

3. What details were most helpful to you to understand the problems Charles Clark is experiencing?

_____

_____

_____

_____

4. What model of mental disorder is the mental health professional using in the assessment, descriptions, and recommendations for treatment?

_____

_____

_____

_____

5. Describe where you see possibilities of stereotyping or bias in the assessment report.

_____

_____

_____

_____

6. What part do you think that multicultural factors might play in the assessment process and the recommendations?

_____

_____

_____

_____

Exercise 6: Using Web Resources

Case managers need information about mental illnesses as they read case files and work with their clients. Numerous web resources provide reliable information about mental illness incidence, detailed descriptions of mental illnesses, vulnerable populations, and possible assessments and treatments. One of the most trustworthy mental health organizations is the National Institute of Mental Health (NIMH), a part of the federal government's National Institutes of Health (NIH), and a branch of the U.S. Department of Health and Human Services. Return to the NIMH website you found in the previous exercise. The following questions help you explore the information available on the NIMH site.

1. What is the purpose of NIMH?

_____

_____

_____

2. What types of mental illnesses are described in detail on the site?

_____

_____

_____

3. Choose one of the illnesses and provide a summary of the disorder, including definition, criteria for diagnosis, incidence, vulnerable populations, and recommended treatments.

_____

_____

_____

_____

4. Find one of the latest reports published by NIMH. What is the topic? Why was it written?

_____

_____

_____

_____

5. Describe at least two areas of research that the NIMH is supporting. Why do you think that this research is important?

_____

_____

_____

_____

••••••• ● Self-Assessment

1. Assume that you are a case manager working with Charles Clark (The case is on the website that accompanies this book, Chapter 7, Link 1.) Discuss in detail how you would approach a physician to request a physical exam. Include a summary of the case and a rationale for the request.

_____

_____

_____

_____

_____

_____

2. Describe your personal and professional encounters with the following professionals. Based upon this description, describe your thoughts about working with each. There may be some professionals for whom you have little information.

Physician:

_____

_____

_____

Social worker:

_____

_____

_____

Psychologist:

_____

_____

_____

Counselor:

_____

_____

_____

3. What information would you like to have about mental disorders before you become a case manager?

_____

_____

_____

 **Pretest Answers**

1. Medical information: Describes functional limitations and potential for rehabilitation; indicates a disease, condition, or poor health that may affect service delivery; provides important social/psychological aspects of the case (p. 163).
2. Hypothermia: word root, combining form, suffix and prefix. Prefix is "hypo" meaning below or under, word root is "therm" meaning heat, suffix is "ia" meaning condition, and the combining form is "othermia" (pp. 167, 170).
3. Strategies: Clarify the need for documentation, use specific questions to help focus on problem, discuss case before evaluation, and prepare the client by explaining the purpose and procedures of the evaluation (p. 175).
4. Social history: Advantages: provides a complete picture of history, appropriate services, and detailed information for future referrals; assesses needs thoroughly; fulfills legal requirements; and builds a relationship: influences clients' perceptions of relationship and may lead to premature judgments and an inaccurate view of relationship, also time consuming; exhaustive histories aren't necessary to plan delivery of services (p. 185).
5. Client's role: Providing vocational information (p. 200), a social history (p. 185), and general information to complete the case file.

References

Cockerham, W. C. (2006). *Sociology of mental disorder* (7th ed.). Upper Saddle River, NJ: Pearson/Prentice Hall.

Fauman, M. A. (2002). *Study guide to DSM-IV-TR*. Washington, DC: American Psychiatric Association Publishing.

Hartman, D. E. (1998). Missed diagnoses and misdiagnoses of environmental toxicant exposure: The psychiatry of toxic exposure and multiple chemical sensitivity. *Psychiatric Clinics of North America, 21*(3), 659–670.

Horwitz, A. (2002). *Creating mental illness*. Chicago: University of Chicago Press.

Morrison, J. (1995). *DSM-IV made easy*. New York: Guilford.

National Institute of Mental Health. (2003). Attention deficit hyperactivity disorder. Retrieved November 19, 2005, from http://www.nimh.nih.gov/publicat/adhd.cfm#symptoms.

National Institute of Mental Health. (2002). Incidence statistics for types of mental illness: Wrong diagnosis. Retrieved November 20, 2005, from http://www.wrongdiagnosis.com/m/mental_illness/incidence-types.htm.

Neighbors, H. W., Trierweiler, B. F., & Muroff, J. R. (2003). Racial differences in the Diagnostic and Statistical Manual diagnosis using a semi-structured instrument: The importance of clinical judgment in the diagnosis of African Americans. *Journal of Health and Social Behavior, 44*, 237–256.

Sorenson, M. J., Mors, O., & Thomsen, P. H. (2005). DSM-IV or ICD-10-DCR diagnoses in child and adolescent psychiatry: Does it matter? *European Child and Adolescent Psychiatry, 14*(6), 335–340.

Spitzer, R. L., & Wilson, P. T. (1975). Nosology and the official psychiatric nomenclature. In A. Freedman, H. Kaplan, and B. Sadock (Eds.), *Comprehensive textbook of psychiatry* (Vol. 1, 2nd ed., pp. 826–845). Baltimore: Williams & Wilkins.

Szasz, T. (1987). *Insanity*. New York: Wiley.

Walker, B. S., & Spengler, P. M. (1995). Clinical judgment of major depression in AIDS patients: The effects of clinician complexity and stereotyping. *Professional Psychology Research and Practice, 26*(3), 269–273.

Whitley, R. (2005). Cultural diversity, mental health and psychiatry: The struggle against racism. *Transcultural Psychiatry, 42*(3), 507–509.

Service Coordination

Following plan development, case managers have two responsibilities. One is to provide direct services; a second is to coordinate services supplied by other staff, other agencies, or both. This chapter focuses on the second, service coordination, and related skills. These include making referrals, monitoring service delivery, working with other professionals, being an advocate, and teaming with others. This chapter provides opportunities for you to develop your own skills in these areas.

 **Pretest**

After you read Chapter 8 in *Generalist Case Management,* answer the following questions and complete the items.

1. List three advantages of service coordination.

_____

_____

_____

2. How can a client participate in service coordination?

_____

_____

_____

3. Define referral.

_____

_____

_____

4. Distinguish between coordinating services and monitoring services.

_____

_____

_____

5. List the six guidelines that lead to successful advocacy.

_____

_____

_____

_____

_____

_____

6. How do the following teams differ?

Treatment team: _____

_____

_____

Departmental team: _____

_____

_____

Interdisciplinary team: _____

_____

_____

Team with family and friends as members: _____

_____

_____

·········●··· Chapter Summary

Although case managers have been providers of direct services in the past, one of the most important responsibilities of case managers today is the coordination of services. Rarely can one person or one agency meet all of the needs of a client. Because of this, the case manager will locate needed resources in the community, arrange for the client to use them, and support the client in using them. Once the case manager and client have agreed upon a plan, then the case manager will locate appropriate resources and make referrals to service providers. The case manager is responsible for documenting throughout the process and should also monitor service delivery to ensure that the client's needs are being met.

While coordinating services, the case manager maintains working relationships with other professionals. Good communication skills are vital during this process. Maintaining appropriate, professional communication with service providers will help meet the needs of the client and any future clients that might require the services of that professional. Often, clients cannot articulate what they need and do not understand what choices are available to them. Case managers might find themselves assuming the role of advocate in their attempts to locate and acquire services for their clients. In this role, the case manager should keep in mind the needs of the client and the other parties involved and develop a clear plan for the client. Because a number of professionals often provide services for a client, teamwork is common. Using teams improves the delivery of services for clients with multiple needs and increases the number of available resources.

·········●··· Exercise 1: Janis Jones

Review the case of Janis Jones in Exercise 2 of Chapter 7. In Chapter 7, you identified Janis's problems, encouraged her participation in plan development, and anticipated barriers to service delivery.

Goal 1 of the plan follows. Review it and respond to the questions that follow it.

THE PLAN

CLIENT: <u>Janis Jones</u>_____ AGE: <u>12</u>

PROBLEM: <u>unruly and violent behavior, possible drug involvement</u>

GOAL 1: <u>To collect additional information to complete picture of present situation.</u>

> **Objective:** <u>To interview the client's teacher about educational performance</u>
>
> **By (date):** <u>4 weeks</u>   Responsible Person: Case Manager
>
> **Objective:** <u>To prepare a social history on the client based on interviews with grandmother and mother during a home visit</u>
>
> **By (date):** <u>3 weeks</u>   Responsible Person: <u>Case Manager</u>
>
> **Objective:** <u>To arrange for a medical examination (make appt.)</u>
>
> **By (date):** <u>2 weeks</u>   Responsible Person: <u>Case Manager</u>
>
> **Objective:** <u>To refer for a psychological evaluation</u>
>
> **By (date):** <u>2 weeks</u>   Responsible Person: <u>Case Manager</u>

1. How will you encourage Janis's participation in reaching the goal?

_____

_____

_____

2. How will you make the referrals? Do you anticipate any barriers? Explain.

_____

_____

_____

_____

3. How will you monitor service provision? What is YOUR plan?

_____

_____

_____

Goal:

_____

_____

_____

Objectives:

_____

_____

_____

_____

4. Describe the criteria you will use for the evaluation of service provision.

_____

_____

_____

_____

5. Describe a situation where you will advocate for Janis.

_____

_____

_____

_____

6. Will you be a broker or a mobilizer? Explain.

_____

_____

_____

_____

············· Exercise 2: Working with Other Professionals

To meet Goal 1, you as the case manager will work with other professionals, including a psychologist (psychological evaluation), social worker (social history), physician (physical examination), and principals, school counselors, and teachers (educational information).

1. What will you tell them about Janis?

_____

_____

_____

_____

2. What questions do you have for each professional to guide his or her evaluation of Janis or your data collection?

Psychologist: _____

_____

_____

_____

_____

Social Worker: _____

_____

_____

_____

_____

Physician: _____

_____

_____

_____

_____

Principal: _____

_____

_____

_____

_____

School Counselor: _____

_____

_____

_____

_____

Teachers: _____

_____

_____

_____

_____

············· Exercise 3: Making a Referral

1. Go to the website that accompanies this book: www.thomsonedu.com/counseling/mcclam, Chapter 8, Link 1, and listen to Iris Jones.
2. Using the information provided in Link 1, identify two problems that Iris is experiencing.
3. Assume that your job as a case manager is to provide Iris the services she needs through referral. Also assume that Iris lives in the city or town in which you currently reside. Using the telephone book, the web, a directory of social services, and colleagues and fellow students, identify at least one agency that might provide the services Iris needs for each problem you listed in item 2. Find out the following information about the agency.

   a. What is the purpose of the agency?

   _____

   _____

   _____

   b. What services does the agency provide?

   _____

   _____

   _____

   c. What is the target population?

   _____

   _____

   _____

   d. What are the eligibility criteria to receive services?

   _____

   _____

   _____

   e. What process is available for making referrals?

   _____

   _____

   _____

Exercise 4: Monitoring Iris's Progress

Assume that you referred Iris to the agency you investigated in Exercise 3.

1. Write a summary of Iris's encounter with this agency from Iris's point of view. Use your readings and experiences to create this encounter.

_____

_____

_____

_____

_____

_____

_____

_____

_____

_____

2. Based upon the summary of Iris's encounter, answer the following questions that will help you, as the case manager, monitor the services Iris is receiving.

   Review of Services

   a. Is Iris receiving services? What services is she receiving?

   _____

   _____

   _____

   b. Is Iris satisfied with the services she is receiving and with her interaction with the agency's staff?

   _____

   _____

   _____

   Changing Conditions

   a. Has Iris's situation changed? How?

   _____

   _____

   _____

   b. Do the services she is receiving reflect the changing conditions? How?

   _____

   _____

   _____

Evaluating Progress

a. Has the problem changed? How?

_____

_____

_____

b. Has there been any resolution to the problems?

_____

_____

_____

c. Should the case be closed? Why or why not?

_____

_____

_____

● Exercise 5: Teamwork

Working with teams is an excellent way to help clients receive quality services. Below are short vignettes of teams that support service delivery. For each vignette, describe what you believe is the primary role of the team and how the client benefits from the team approach.

Team A

Five professionals are gathered together to consider cases of four adolescents arrested for first-time possession of cocaine. The judge from juvenile court refers offenders to the case management team for assessment and services instead of incarceration. The professionals include a family specialist from the department of human services, a probation officer, a psychologist, a mental health counselor serving as the case manager, and a school liaison.

_____

_____

_____

_____

_____

Team B

Lakewood Hills, Inc. provides support services for Alzheimer's patients and their families. Each patient and family is assigned a case manager who spearheads the service delivery. Each week the case manager chairs a discussion with other professionals who provide an array of services such as physical care, home health services, respite care, and educational services that foster positive psychological development for patients and caregivers.

_____

_____

_____

_____

_____

<u>Team C</u>

Family members participate in a group cooperative that they have formed themselves. Each family has at least one member with a persistent mental illness. As a result of the families' cooperative, they are able to advocate for their family members. To date, they provide a group day care, organize outings to the mall and movies, dispense medications daily, and coordinate time for caretakers to take days off from care giving. The cooperative hired one case manager, who works two hours a day to advise and support these efforts of the families.

_____

_____

_____

_____

_____

•••••••••••••• In More Depth: Advocacy Beyond the Individual Level

Chapter 8 focuses on advocacy at the client level. This means speaking on behalf of clients whether pleading their case or standing up for their rights. An example of the case manager's roles and responsibilities at this level is Stan.

> The case manager met Stan at the hospital emergency room following treatment for a suicide attempt. Stan is a cross-dresser who is narcissistic and currently planning operations and hormone therapy to become female. He is also in denial about his AIDS and impending death. Stan is going to be discharged from the emergency room in two hours. The challenge the case manager faces is finding a shelter that will accept a male who looks female and has AIDS.

In addition to the immediate problem of finding a place for Stan to stay this very night, there is a broader issue here: the resistance of three different emergency shelters to accept Stan for temporary housing. This reality reflects the perceptions and attitudes of shelter staff and governing boards about the gay, lesbian, bisexual, and transgender community (GLBT) and people with AIDS.

The dilemma faced by community agencies in a major urban center in the United States is another example of the need for advocacy beyond the client level. Newly proposed state regulations for a single point of access to client services left many staff at these community agencies confused and angry about their implementation. Staff members at these agencies are unprepared, lack knowledge about resources, and are concerned about coordination. If you could talk with these staff members, they would tell you that no one knows better than they do about their clients' needs and an agency's services. Yet they had no voice in the development of these new regulations. They will be primarily responsible for implementing these regulations and resent the fact that they were not part of the planning process. So there are several problems here. One is that those charged with following this new system don't understand it. Second, this same group is integral to its success. Finally, those who know best what the issues and challenges are for themselves and their clients have no voice in this change. They want to know how they can be part of the process—or any future process where changes are planned.

Both of these examples call for advocacy at a level different from individual advocacy. The purpose of advocacy at the agency, community, state, or federal level is to promote change in any number of areas: for example, legislation, rules and regulations, policies, statutes, budgets, and attitudes. Participants may be any or all of the following: case managers and other human service professionals, clients, and community representatives and volunteers.

Why aren't we better advocates at this level when we would probably all agree it is needed? There are many reasons for this. One in a very practical sense is lack of time. With large caseloads, accountability demands, and clients with multiple problems, many professionals recognize that advocacy is necessary but time for this activity is a luxury. For others, it is a lack of know-how.

How exactly does one go about advocating at this level? Many know how to speak for their clients or represent the needs of their clients in such a way that clients receive what they need. But advocacy at these more complex levels requires different skills, and case managers rarely have training in this area. Another problem is that many agencies and organizations discourage staff from drawing media attention, particularly that which is negative, to themselves or the agency unless sanctioned by the administration. There is often a chain of command in place that must be consulted prior to any publicity. Finally, advocacy is frequently absent from any job description or job responsibilities. So there are a number of reasons for the lack of advocacy at levels greater than individual client advocacy.

One way to increase advocacy efforts is to understand the advocacy process and the skills necessary for success in this area. The process begins with the identification of a problem or a need. A temporary shelter for Stan is a problem at the client level. A broader issue is the need to increase sensitivity and services to the GLBT community. Following this initial step is the identification of targets, the entity that needs change— that is, the shelter staff, board of directors, or community. Planning is the third step. Ezell (2001) identifies four strategies named for the area in which they occur as well as the location of targets for change: agency advocacy, legislative advocacy, legal advocacy, and community advocacy. The final step is implementation of the plan.

This fourth step focuses on the use of skills that are action oriented. They include monitoring proposals, laws, policies, and practices; educating staff, clients, the community, the public, legislators, and officials; lobbying/campaigning for candidates, ideas, or both by writing letters and using the media; and organizing constituents, coalitions, agencies, and networks.

If we examine each of the four strategies, then it is clear how these skills can be applied. The first is agency advocacy. This involves areas such as policies, budgets, and practices. For example, some practices may be unfair or unhelpful to clients, the staff, or the community and other needed practices may be nonexistent, so monitoring services and programs, educating the people affected, and working with others are ways to promote any necessary changes.

Legislative advocacy requires understanding the legislative process described in Chapter 2. Effectiveness in this type of advocacy is knowing how to sell or promote your idea to a legislator, gathering support for it, and moving it through a committee or a floor vote. Lobbying skills are also often necessary. Although lobbying usually refers to persuading a local or state legislator or member of Congress to vote a certain way, staff members often lobby an administrator or board of directors to change policies and procedures. The Americans with Disabilities Act is an example of a successful effort to enact legislation that guarantees equal rights to people with disabilities and prevents discrimination against them.

Legal advocacy involves two approaches (Ezell, 2001). One is not litigious, which means that this approach is unrelated to filing lawsuits; the other involves litigation. Generally, this type of advocacy is related to the practice of law and the courts; however, it may also include both agency and legislative advocacy. Examples of successful legal advocacy that involved litigation include the right to treatment or to refuse treatment in mental health settings, the right of clients to be placed in least restrictive environments, and the right to equal educational opportunities. An example of nonlitigious tactics is the identification of situations where clients' rights may have been violated. In these cases, an effective advocate can assist clients in identifying when this is occurring and what resources or legal assistance is available to them.

Finally, community advocacy is a fourth strategy to change ideas and attitudes. For example, misinformation or inaccurate beliefs may be driving the adoption of a particular program or a legislative proposal. In some states, efforts are underway to prevent gays and lesbians from marrying or adopting children. In most areas, local, state, and national organizations are working for the rights of same-sex couples to marry and to adopt children. These organizations support legal defense funds, activities of lobbyists, and educational programs. These efforts support human rights and basic civil liberties. The case of Stan also illustrates the need to work with shelter staffs, governing boards, and the larger community to change attitudes and accessibility to services. There are a number of ways to educate communities with correct information: for example, interviews, letters to the editor, op-ed pieces, press conferences, presentations, and mailings. A more recent development is the use of technology to disseminate information and to educate the citizenry via the Internet and e-mails.

Case Study: Casita Maria

Casita Maria is a settlement house in the South Bronx. A staff of 15 provided social services in homeless intervention, homeless placement, immigration issues, and job training until 9/11. Following 9/11, the $376,000 budget was cut to $40,000. Most of its funding was from the city, and budget cuts and a focus on fighting terrorism have impacted its budget. Now, one caseworker tries to handle as much as she can in a day: a senior who cannot write and needs some money orders to pay bills; an abused woman who is ready to leave her situation; an illegal immigrant who wants to return home; new immigrant groups, including Mexicans, Ecuadorians, Hondurans, and Africans, with myriad problems; and new gangs like the Mexican gang and the Dominican gang that are attracting teenagers and young adults.

In addition to those problems, workers are also facing challenges. Marta Rivera recounted the experience of one worker prior to 9/11 (and the reduction of staff at the agency) who had a heart attack during a home visit and died. She used to go out in the field by herself. Marta believes in the buddy system on home visits, but sometimes it isn't possible due to staffing limitations. This colleague actually passed away in an elevator by herself with just a beeper. Staff decided to go on strike, refusing to go into the field alone, knowing that the problem could be fixed or they could be terminated. But it was clear they would have to fight for a change. And a change is what they got: The buddy system became policy. Shortly after this change, another worker was walking by a construction site when something fell and hit her leg. She was hospitalized for over a week, then in a brace for three months. Because she was with a buddy, the office was notified immediately and a staff member met them at the hospital. This is a good system in an urban area where some clients seem to think you are either the police or a Child Welfare worker and you're the enemy.

Following the budget cuts after 9/11, the agency shifted from social services to education. For example, the agency is sponsoring an immigration forum this month. Planning is also underway for a gang awareness evening for the entire community, particularly parents. A partnership has been established with the American Ballet Theater, which visits Casita Maria to teach ballet to children in the community. In addition to ballet, the children are learning discipline and responsibility. They are also planning a story to dance, designing costumes, and learning about lighting and stage sets.

············● Exercise 6: Advocacy and Casita Maria

As you think about advocacy beyond the individual level, respond to the following questions:

1. If you were a staff member at Casita Maria after 9/11, what would you advocate for?

_____

_____

_____

_____

2. How would you advocate for the agency?

_____

_____

_____

_____

3. An increase in gang activity is a community concern. Think about ways to address the problem and the role of advocacy in addressing it.

_____

_____

_____

_____

● Exercise 7: Advocacy and Stan

Suppose you are the case manager who works with Stan. The lack of services or the unwillingness of services to assist clients like Stan indicates a larger community problem. How might you use each of these three strategies to help with this situation?

Community advocacy:

_____

_____

_____

_____

Legislative advocacy:

_____

_____

_____

_____

Legal advocacy:

_____

_____

_____

_____

● Exercise 8: Advocacy and You

  1. How might you employ each of the following action-oriented skills?

Monitoring:

_____

_____

_____

_____

Educating:

_____

_____

_____

_____

Lobbying/campaigning:

_____

_____

_____

_____

Organizing:

_____

_____

_____

_____

2. Identify a problem that you've encountered at your school (parking, financial aid, rules and regulations, not enough courses, and so on). Using your skills, develop an advocacy plan to address this problem. Include the four strategies introduced here and the skills you would use to implement your plan.

_____

_____

_____

_____

_____

_____

Self-Assessment

1. How important do you think advocacy is?

_____

_____

_____

2. How comfortable do you think you will be in the advocacy role?

_____

_____

_____

3. How will you develop your skills in this area?

_____

_____

_____

_____

Pretest Answers

1. Three advantages of coordination: client gets access to an array of services, case manager's knowledge and skills help client gain access to needed services, and effective and efficient service delivery is promoted (p. 212).
2. Client participation: determining the problem, calling for assistance, identifying values / strengths / interests play a role in selecting resources, getting referrals, and providing written consent for confidentiality (p. 213).

3. Referral: connects the client with a resource within the agency structure or at another agency (p. 216).
4. Monitoring of services: review of services received, conditions that may have changed, extent of progress toward goals and objectives (p. 219).
5. Guidelines: 1. know the environment in which the conflict takes place, 2. understand the needs of the client and of the other parties involved, 3. develop a clear plan for the client, 4. use techniques of persuasion when appropriate, 5. write or state agreement, once it is obtained, and 6. use more adversarial techniques when persuasion proves ineffective (pp. 226–227).
6. Teams: Treatment team (p. 229), coordinated team for multiple problems who review the problems, evaluate information and make recommendations. Departmental team (p. 230), act as support, bring in challenging cases to help identify problems and generate alternatives, share information and make group decisions. Interdisciplinary team (p. 230), representatives of services received includes client and one family member who share data, establish goals and develop plan then monitor progress with case manager as team leader. Family and Friends team (p. 232), contribute input and participate in planning and all other phases of case management, expand the network of support as part of the solution, add perspectives on environment and needs, but may not be supportive.

 # Reference

Ezell, M. (2001). *Advocacy in the human services.* Belmont, CA: Thomson/Brooks/Cole.

Chapter 9

Working with the Organizational Context

M any times case management takes place within an agency or organization. The organizational context influences the climate in which individuals work and the way in which services are delivered. This organizational context, the subject of Chapter 9, *Generalist Case Management*, describes the organizational structure, agency resources, and how to improve services. This chapter provides opportunities for you to develop your skills in these areas. The following pretest reviews concepts relating to organizational structure and environment introduced in Chapter 9.

 **Pretest**

After you read Chapter 9 in *Generalist Case Management,* answer the following questions and complete the items.

1. What are three key concepts that the case manager must master to understand the organization? Why is each helpful?

_____

_____

_____

_____

_____

2. Describe the purpose of a mission statement and outline its components.

_____

_____

_____

_____

_____

3. How do the concepts of authority, accountability, and chain of command relate to one another?

_____

_____

_____

_____

_____

4. Describe four ways that the formal and informal structures of an agency differ.

_____

_____

_____

_____

5. Define organizational climate.

_____

_____

_____

_____

_____

Chapter Summary

Case management, in most cases, occurs within the context of an organization. The structure of the organization often reflects the goals, policies, and mission of the agency. Understanding the organizational structure allows case managers to more effectively provide services for their clients. The way an organization is structured is often described in the agency's mission statement, as well as other documents. A mission statement summarizes the guiding principles of the agency, describes the populations that benefit from its work, and specifies the values that guide the work of the staff. Agencies generally have a formal structure that details the relationships among people and departments, who has authority for certain decisions, who is accountable for resources, and the chain of command in the organization. An organizational chart is a symbolic representation of the lines of authority and accountability, as well as the communication flow within the organization. Agencies also have informal structures that usually develop as ways to meet agency needs that the formal structure fails to meet. The case manager must distinguish between the formal structure and the informal structure. The organizational climate influences how case managers perform their jobs and relate to their clients, and it usually reflects the attitudes, values, and feelings of people in the agency.

The agency's policies and procedures determine the amount of involvement that case managers have in planning a budget, but regardless of the level of involvement in planning the budget, it is important for case managers to understand the basic concepts of budgeting. Some case managers are directly involved in budgeting for their individual clients. Case managers should be aware of resource allocation issues at the organizational level and resource allocation policies for individual clients. Utilization review by managed care organizations often helps determine the best use of resources in light of the anticipated outcomes. Because limited funds are allotted for each client, it is critical to assess client needs and the cost of relevant services before providing such services. Managed care organizations use the utilization review process to improve the overall quality of services. Quality assurance programs are also developed in an effort to improve treatment standards and client satisfaction.

Exercise 1: Writing a Mission Statement

By this time you have been studying case management for several weeks. You have received a syllabus, completed a few assignments, and participated in class discussion and activities. Based on these activities, can you determine the mission of this course?

1. Write a mission statement that reflects your classroom experience.

_____

_____

_____

_____

_____

_____

_____

2. Did your mission statement for the course include:

   - Primary Goals   YES   NO
   - Primary Values   YES   NO
   - Primary Outcomes/Constituencies to Receive Services   YES   NO

Rewrite your mission statement for the course so that it includes goals, values, and outcomes for the class members.

_____

_____

_____

_____

_____

_____

_____

_____

3. Is the mission statement for the course compatible with its goals and objectives? Describe why or why not.

_____

_____

_____

_____

4. Is the mission statement for the course compatible with classroom readings and assignments? Describe why or why not.

_____

_____

_____

_____

5. Share your mission statement for the class with your instructor.

·············● Exercise 2: The Job Description

In Chapter 9, "Working Within the Organizational Context," in *Generalist Case Management*, you read about Carlotta's experiences as a case manager. To review Carlotta's experience, either re-read Chapter 9 or go to the website that accompanies this book: www.thomsonedu.com/counseling/mcclam, Chapter 9, Link 1.

1. Based upon the information provided, write a job description for Carlotta. Be sure to include a job summary, a list of responsibilities, a list of expected outcomes, and the nature of supervision received.

_____

_____

_____

_____

_____

_____

_____

Exercise 3: Formal and Informal Structure

Within all organizations there exists a formal structure within which employees are expected to work. Parallel to this formal structure is an alternative, informal way of getting things accomplished. Read the following excerpts from interviews with case managers in a variety of agencies. After each excerpt identify and describe the informal structure, the formal structure, or both.

Excerpt 1

Then there's case management supervision. Each case manager meets regularly with his or her supervisor to discuss any issues that they have on their agenda, to discuss different approach methods or intervention models.

_____

_____

_____

_____

Excerpt 2

Something often happens here. A client comes to us after she or he have been through a series of systems and nobody has ever pulled it together. This is a place where the staff is still connected. That's why services and the connection between services and housing are so important. Because you deal with clients and with what the issues are. And these are people who have been through the system and they are so skilled at going into the office and presenting themselves. They know exactly how to walk into each individual agency and talk to the case manager. I remember we had one client early on, who, when we tracked it down, had 16 different agencies, including a private lawyer. And she was playing them all off against the other and nobody, until she came here, had ever said, "Let's all sit down and see what she's telling each of us."

_____

_____

_____

_____

Excerpt 3

I had a young man who came here because he didn't know what to do. He came by himself. He has no relatives here. He is a very young guy, maybe 22, 23 years old, and he wanted to make it here so he could send for his family. But he came illegally. So he found himself working in a grocery store 50 or 60 hours a week for $150, and that's not what he wanted. That's not the American dream to him, so he came in. He had saved enough money and return home. He asked me, "How can I go back without getting in any trouble? Because I can't go back the way I came in. There's no way," he said. "But I have money. I saved everything that I made." So I made arrangements for him to leave on a plane. First of all, I made a connection with a friend of mine who runs a travel agency, and I told him exactly the truth. "This guy is here illegally and he needs to go back legally—how can we make this happen?" He says, "He needs to make sure that he has proper ID, because they will document this, that he left, in the event that he comes back." And I told him, "Give me a break with this guy. He has no money. Give me whatever is the cheapest; it doesn't make a difference if it's four o'clock in the morning. If he has any money, I'd like him at least to take it with him."

_____

_____

_____

_____

Exercise 4: Critique Ways of "Doing Business"

Review the excerpts in Exercise 3 and the examples you identified for the formal and the informal structures. For each excerpt, evaluate the strengths and limitations of using the formal or the informal structure to get things done.

Excerpt 1:

_____

_____

_____

_____

_____

Excerpt 2:

_____

_____

_____

_____

_____

Excerpt 3:

_____

_____

_____

_____

_____

Exercise 5: Work-Related Values

1. Rate the importance of each of the following in terms of the job you want in human services.

   4 = most important to me
   3 = important, but not a top priority
   2 = slightly important
   1 = of little or no importance

   _____ 1. High salary; a job with economic growth possibilities.

   _____ 2. Leadership, authority, and influence over others.

   _____ 3. A job with status; to be held in high esteem by peers.

   _____ 4. Protection against sudden job loss or layoff.

   _____ 5. Diversity of work tasks.

   _____ 6. Able to be self-reliant and self-regulating.

   _____ 7. Balance between family and job.

_____ 8. Work that appeals to me.

_____ 9. Opportunity to help others.

_____ 10. Stimulation on the job.

_____ 11. Innovation; opportunity to be creative on the job.

_____ 12. Satisfaction gained through work.

_____ 13. Collaboration with other professionals.

_____ 14. Competition with others.

_____ 15. Promotion opportunities.

_____ 16. Professional development opportunities.

2. How will you match what's important to you with a job description?

_____

_____

_____

_____

3. Go to the website that accompanies this book, Chapter 9, Link 2, to hear Sharon describe what she likes best about her job. Identify the three values in item 1 that she would choose as most important for herself.

_____

_____

Exercise 6: Budgeting

The following budget represents expenditures for a volunteer training program at a statewide agency.

Salaries

Position	Percentage of Time	Amount
Director	100%	50,000
Volunteer Coordinator	50%	15,000
Curriculum Development Specialist	50%	13,000
Secretary	100%	15,500
Total Salaries		**$93,000**

Equipment
(prices taken from Office Max website and ProjectorCenter.com)

Computer	1,099
Software (e.g., Microsoft Office & McAfee)	449
Recorder/Transcriber	200
Laptop	1,499
Proxima	1,599
Total Equipment Costs	**$4,846**

Supplies

General Office Supplies	1,000
Total Supplies	**$1,000**

Staff Travel

Travel to 2 national conferences @1,000/trip × 2 trips	2,000
Per diem: $46/day × 8 days	368
Local Travel: 200 miles/month × 32¢/miles × 12 months	768
Total Staff Travel	**$3,136**

Other Expenses

Expense	Amount
Telephone	3,000
Postage: $55/month × 12 months	660
Duplication	1,250
Total Other Expenses	**$4,910**

Trainee Expenses

Books: $19.95 × 30 trainees	598.55
Meals: $8.95/day × 30 trainees × 2 days	537.00
Training Manuals: Printing/Reproduction for 30 @$15.50 ea.	465.00
Total Trainee Expenses	**$1,655.55**

Board Meetings (15 members)

Duplication	150
Food	85
Total Board Expenses	**$235**

Consultants

Visiting Lecturers (2 @ 1,000/day)	2,000
Evaluation consultant: 5 hrs @$250/hour	1,250
Per diem: $46/day × 2 lecturers	92
Total Consultant Costs	**$3,342**

1. Review the budget. Are you surprised at any items?

_____

_____

_____

_____

2. Suppose you are a board member. Are there any categories or expenses you would question?

_____

_____

_____

_____

3. The board has just mandated a 33 percent cut in the budget. How would you accomplish this? Use the following worksheet to outline revisions.

_____

_____

_____

_____

Budget Worksheet

Salaries

Position	Percentage of Time	Amount	Proposed Revisions
Director	100%	50,000	
Volunteer Coordinator	50%	15,000	
Curriculum Development Specialist	50%	13,000	
Secretary	100%	15,500	
Total Salaries		**$93,000**	

Equipment

		Amount	Proposed Revisions
Computer		1,099	
Software (e.g., Microsoft Office & McAfee)		449	
Recorder/Transcriber		200	
Laptop		1,499	
Proxima		1,599	
Total Equipment Costs		**$4,846**	

Supplies

	Amount	Proposed Revisions
General Office Supplies	1,000	
Total Supplies	**$1,000**	

Staff Travel

	Amount	Proposed Revisions
Travel to 2 national conferences @ 1,000/trip × 2 trips	2,000	
Per diem: $46/day × 8 days	368	
Local Travel: 200 miles/month × 32¢/miles × 12 months	768	
Total Staff Travel	**$3,136**	

Other Expenses

	Amount	Proposed Revision
Telephone	3,000	
Postage: $55/month × 12 months	660	
Duplication	1,250	
Total Other Expenses	**$4,910**	

Trainee Expenses

	Amount	Proposed Revision
Books: $19.95 × 30 trainees	598.55	
Meals: $8.95/day × 30 trainees × 2 days	537.00	
Training Manuals: Printing/Reproduction for 30 @$15.50 ea.	465.00	
Total Trainee Expenses	**$1,655.55**	

Board Meetings (15 members)

	Amount	Proposed Revision
Duplication	150	
Food	85	
Total Board Expenses	**$235**	

Consultants

	Amount	Proposed Revision
Visiting Lecturers (2 @ 1,000/day)	2,000	
Evaluation consultant: 5 hrs @$250/hour	1,250	
Per diem: $46/day × 2 lecturers	92	
Total Consultant Costs	**$3,342**	

············● In More Depth: Looking from the Outside In

You met Carlotta in Chapter 9 of *Generalist Case Management*. She has been working for the Sexual Assault Crisis Center as a case manager. She is now deciding whether to leave her job. Rather than walk out on the job and her clients because she has had a bad day or she has a little success with several clients, she decides to go to a career counselor for help. The process the career counselor uses has one purpose: to help clients, in this case Carlotta, think through their relationships with the agencies where they work. The career counselor believes that there should be a match between the organization and the individual. Let's see how the counselor works with Carlotta.

Carlotta begins her discussion by summarizing the things that have happened to her since she took this job. Basically she provides the same information you read from the website that accompanies this book, Chapter 9, Line 1.

The counselor uses a set of three questions to help a client assess the relationship with the agency: Why did I take the job? What is the working environment like? Should I stay or leave?

Question 1: Why did I take the job?

Carlotta filled out the following survey including the questions at the end of the survey. By the time she completed the form, she thought she understood more about herself and why she took the job. Following is the survey with Carlotta's responses.

TAKING THE JOB

Please answer the following items focused on your thinking at the time you took the job.

5 = strongly agree, 3 = agree, 1 = strongly disagree, and UA = unaware.

ITEM:	RESPONSES:			
1. Both the organization and I will benefit if I take this job.	(5)	3	1	UA
2. My values and the organization's values are similar.	(5)	3	1	UA
3. I want to help the organization reach its mission and goals.	(5)	3	1	UA
4. The agency and I are committed to helping a population in need.	(5)	3	1	UA
5. I believe the organization will provide me resources to support my work.	(5)	3	1	UA
6. The agency views me as a professional.	(5)	3	1	UA
7. I trust the agency to fulfill its promises to me.	(5)	3	1	UA
8. The agency and I agree on my job roles and responsibilities.	(5)	3	1	UA
9. I believe I will contribute to agency planning.	(5)	3	1	UA
10. The agency promises that I will be able to make my own decisions with regard to clients.	(5)	3	1	UA

Please answer the following questions.

What information did you gather before you accepted the job?

I probably did not ask enough questions about the organization. I have always wanted to work with women and children in crisis, building on my experience in college, and I was thrilled to have an interview. Quite frankly, I only read the job description.

How did you feel about the job prior to signing a contract?

I was so excited but I also remember my first days and the week before I took the job. I was afraid that I could not do the job. My focus was really only on me, the job, and the clients. I never thought much about the organization. When I interview for my next job, I will ask the questions on this survey.

•••••••••••• Exercise 7: Taking the Job

Review Carlotta's story and her responses to the "Taking the Job" survey and answer the following questions.

1. Describe how Carlotta viewed the organizational climate of the agency when she took the job.

_____
_____
_____
_____

2. How did the mission and goals of the agency influence Carlotta's decision to take the job?

_____

_____

_____

_____

3. Using Carlotta's responses to the "Taking the Job" Survey, describe the factors that influenced her decision to work for this agency.

_____

_____

_____

_____

Question 2: What is the working environment like?

The counselor then asked Carlotta to focus on her work experience at the agency. Again she filled out a survey to help clarify what had happened to her as she worked at the Sexual Assault Crisis Center.

•••••••••••• Exercise 8: Assessing the Work Environment

Review Carlotta's responses to "Assessing Your Work Environment" and answer the following questions.

1. In your opinion, what are the strengths of Carlotta's organization?

_____

_____

_____

_____

2. What information about the organization might help Carlotta better understand the working environment?

_____

_____

_____

_____

3. In what ways is Carlotta involved in decision making of the organization?

_____

_____

_____

_____

Question 3: Should I Stay or Leave?

The final component of Carlotta's review with her counselor focuses on whether she should stay with the agency. This survey addresses issues concerned with the climate in which she works. It also helps her articulate what is important to her.

ASSESSING YOUR WORK ENVIRONMENT

Please answer the following items focused on your thinking at the time you took the job.

5 = strongly agree, 3 = agree, 1 = strongly disagree, and UA = unaware.

   1.

ITEM :	RESPONSES:			
1. I am clear about my responsibilities.	5	(3)	1	UA
2. My responsibilities have changed since I began my job.	5	3	(1)	UA
3. Individuals (other than my supervisor) help me when I have questions.	5	3	(1)	UA
4. I have a supervisor.	5	(3)	1	UA
5. I am clear about my supervisor's responsibilities.	5	3	(1)	UA
6. My supervisor is available when I have questions.	5	3	(1)	UA
7. My agency expects me to be available beyond my 40-hour work week.	(5)	3	1	UA
8. When I ask questions my supervisor is helpful.	5	3	(1)	UA
9. I believe I will contribute to agency planning.	5	(3)	1	UA
10. I have an opportunity to discuss issues related to resource allocation.	5	(3)	1	UA
11. Conflict within the agency is addressed.	5	3	(1)	UA
12. I work in an open, honest environment.	5	3	(1)	UA
13. There are always hidden agendas.	5	3	(1)	UA
14. I respect my colleagues.	5	(3)	1	UA

Please answer the following questions.

What do you like most about your job?

I really like my clients. They're in need of my help and I can establish relationships with them. Even though our services are limited I can refer clients to other services. I also liked working with the budget committee.

If you could improve communication in your agency, what would you change?

I wish that I had a stronger supervisor. I spend so much time just wandering around unsure of who to talk to. I was so scared of doing the wrong thing. And I wish people would be more honest and open.

What do you know about the agency's funding?

Working with the budget committee I learned a lot about the budget. I did not have any control, but what a difference funding makes. I love working with the quality effort. It has allowed me to know more people from the agency and understand the agency better. The funding is very complex and although I do not know all about it I do know they have state, federal funds, as well as private donations.

How would you change its allocation resources?

Right now I don't have enough time to work with my clients; in other words, I have too many clients. If I could see them, I could give them more help. This means we would have to reallocate to hire more case managers.

SHOULD I STAY OR LEAVE?

Please answer the following items focused on your thinking at the time you took the job.

5 = strongly agree, 3 = agree, 1 = strongly disagree, and UA = unaware.

ITEM:	RESPONSES:			
1. Planning is important in my organization.	5	(3)	1	UA
2. There is confusion and/or anger because of lack of planning.	5	(3)	1	UA
3. The management is involving us in planning efforts.	5	(3)	1	UA
4. Planning or lack of planning affects my job.	(5)	3	1	UA
5. Planning or lack of planning affects my clients.	(5)	3	1	UA
6. There is good communication within the agency.	5	3	(1)	UA
7. There is a poor communication within the agency.	(5)	3	1	UA
8. There is confusion within the agency because of poor communication.	(5)	3	1	UA
9. Communication or lack of communication affects my job.	(5)	3	1	UA
10. Communication or lack of communication affects service delivery.	(5)	3	1	UA
11. Goals and objectives are clear.	5	(3)	1	UA
12. Resource allocation is linked to goals and objectives.	5	3	(1)	UA
13. There is confusion at the agency because of the lack of clear goals or objectives.	(5)	3	1	UA
14. I am involved in goal setting.	5	(3)	1	UA
15. Goal setting affects service delivery.	(5)	3	1	UA
16. I have too few responsibilities.	5	3	(1)	UA
17. I have overwhelming responsibilities.	(5)	3	1	UA
18. I am confused about my responsibilities.	5	(3)	1	UA
19. My benefits of working here match my responsibilities.	5	3	(1)	UA
20. The number of responsibilities I have affects service delivery.	(5)	3	1	UA
21. I have enough resources to do my job well.	5	(3)	1	UA
22. I do not have enough resources to do my job well.	(5)	3	1	UA
23. I have input into resource allocation.	5	(3)	1	UA
24. I have no input into resource allocation.	5	(3)	1	UA
25. Resource allocation affects service delivery.	(5)	3	1	UA

Please answer the following questions.

Based upon your response to the survey, what is going right with the organization?

I think the organization is truly committed to its clients. And in some ways the organization tries to involve us in its work.

Based upon your response to the survey, what is going wrong in the organization?

There is a lot of communication about policy and procedures I think among the managers, but no one seems to talk with the case managers about these. And sometimes even the managers do not talk to one another. There is also a lack of supervision.

Exercise 9: Should I Stay or Leave?

Review Carlotta's responses to "Should I Stay or Leave?" and answer the following questions:

1. What qualities in an organization seem to be important to Carlotta? How do her responses reflect them?

_____

_____

_____

_____

2. Summarize Carlotta's feelings about the agency based upon her responses to this survey.

_____

_____

_____

_____

Exercise 10: Summary

1. Review the summary of Carlotta's job description, her responses to the three surveys, and your answers to Exercises 7, 8, and 9.

2. The following questions will help you reflect on Carlotta's thoughts and feelings about her job.

   - What are the main points that stand out for you when you read Carlotta's vignette?

_____

_____

_____

_____

   - Why do you think Carlotta took the job as a Sexual Assault Crisis Center case manager?

_____

_____

_____

   - Based upon Carlotta's responses to the three surveys, what did Carlotta like the best and what did she like the least about her job?

_____

_____

_____

_____

3. Use the following terms to explain Carlotta's experience at the Sexual Assault Crisis Center.

   Mission statement:

_____

_____

_____

Job description:

_____

_____

_____

Chain of command:

_____

_____

_____

Formal organizational structure:

_____

_____

_____

Informal organizational structure:

_____

_____

_____

Organizational climate:

_____

_____

_____

Budget:

_____

_____

_____

Sources of revenue:

_____

_____

_____

Improving service:

_____

_____

_____

4. Compare Carlotta's response to "Taking the Job" with "Should I Stay or Leave?" What conclusion can you draw?

_____

_____

_____

5. Should Carlotta stay at the Sexual Assault Crisis Center or should she leave? Make a recommendation and provide a rationale.

_____

_____

_____

_____

Self-Assessment

1. What type of organizational climate would you like to work in?

_____

_____

_____

_____

2. How would you assess the values of the organization in contrast to your own?

_____

_____

_____

_____

3. Why might you remain at an agency? Why might you leave an agency?

_____

_____

_____

_____

Pretest Answers

1. Key concepts: organizational structure; agency resources, and improving services (p. 237).

2. Mission statement: the purpose is to provide guiding principles of the agency. Usually states broad goals, describes specific values, the agency structure, sources of funding, priorities, and work of staff (p. 239).

3. Concepts of authority, accountability, and chain of command: These relate to each other in terms of the structure of the organization. Authority describes responsibilities that are assumed, accountability refers to how those in authority are responsible for particular tasks, and chain of command describes how individuals relate to each other, in terms of authority (p. 241).

4. Differences in informal and formal structure: formal refers to supervision and informal refers to advice giving; formal refers to the job description, informal refers to what the professional actually does; formal refers to the designated lines of communication, informal refers to who actually communicates with whom; formal asks what is the policy, informal asks what actually happens (p. 245).

5. Organization climate: conditions of the work environment (p. 246).

Ethical and Legal Issues

Chapter 10 in *Generalist Case Management* presents ethical and legal considerations that case managers encounter in their professional work. This chapter enables you to work with these issues as you apply them to service delivery.

············ Pretest

When you finish reading Chapter 10 in *Generalist Case Management*, answer the following questions and complete the items.

1. What guidelines might you follow when you are working as a case manager with family disagreements?

_____

_____

_____

2. Describe work situations where the threat of potential violence might be high.

_____

_____

_____

3. Why is confidentiality so difficult to maintain?

_____

_____

_____

4. Define duty to warn.

_____

_____

_____

5. Describe how case managers can support autonomous end-of-life decisions.

_____

_____

_____

············ Chapter Summary

In the case management process, decision making is often complicated by complex ethical and legal issues. In some cases, such as end-of-life issues, family disagreements complicate situations, and the case manager must be prepared to follow the client's wishes and act in the client's best interest as much as possible. In other situations, case managers will find themselves working with potentially violent clients. In these situations, the case manager is responsible for alerting other professionals or individuals involved in caring for the client to the possibility of violence. One of the fundamental responsibilities of any helping professional is the obligation of confidentiality. To develop a helping relationship, the client must be assured that information disclosed during the helping process will be kept in confidence. Even though case managers strive to uphold confidentiality, there are certain circumstances in which confidentiality must be broken. The case manager should discuss the issue of confidentiality early in the helping relationship. As the use of computer technology becomes an integral part of many case managers' work, confidentiality of client records is an important issue. The case manager should take care to safeguard client records and information. Violation of confidentiality is considered unacceptable practice in most instances. One exception to this ethical standard is the case manager's "duty to warn" others if the client is a threat to him- or herself or to others.

Ethical dilemmas may arise for case managers who work with clients in managed care organizations. Because managed care organizations operate within a business atmosphere, case managers who are committed to act in the best interest of their clients often face ethical dilemmas. To work effectively within the managed care context, case managers need to understand that clients may not be able to receive all of the services "they need." Case managers can help clients receive services by writing clear, well-documented treatment plans.

One of the fundamental values of case management is client autonomy. At times, clients' preferences may not be in their best interests. In these situations, case managers may find themselves in a position where client autonomy should be restricted. For case managers working with clients who are at the end of their lives, client autonomy can be strengthened by helping the client establish advance directives. Case managers are often governed by different bodies, such as professional organizations, the law, and their employer. One of the most difficult dilemmas that a case manager can face is whether to comply with laws, regulations, and rules of practice when these do not appear to meet client needs.

•••••••••••••• ● Exercise 1: End-of-Life Care

Chapter 10 in *Generalist Case Management* discusses the complications that may occur when there are family disagreements about the care of clients. These types of disagreements often occur while the client or patient is near the end of life. Specialized training for case managers to support the work of the medical staff and to facilitate communication among the medical staff, the client/patient, and the family is important. Several guidelines for discussing end-of-life care include:

◆ Help the client/patient to discuss concerns, goals, and values with family and medical staff
◆ Acknowledge client/patient feelings and help client/patient determine the meaning of the feelings
◆ Help the client/patient talk about topics that are particularly difficult
◆ Help identify any spiritual issues
◆ Support the client/patient's discussions with family members and with medical staff
   (Lo, Quill, & Tulsky, 2005).

Using these guidelines, answer the questions about your case management responsibilities in the following situation.

You are the case manager for a local hospice organization. Bruno Juskulski, husband of Joyce, has called you to consult about care for his dying wife. They have been married for 53 years. Currently Joyce is hospitalized; the doctors say that there is nothing they can do for her lung cancer; they told Bruno that she is terminally ill. They do not expect her to live for more than two months. Joyce will not talk with Bruno or with any of their three daughters.

1. What do you see as your responsibilities as the case manager?

_____

_____

_____

2. Based on your understanding of your responsibilities described in Question 1, explain how you will use the guidelines provided above to begin a discussion with Joyce.

◆ Try to help the client/patient to discuss concerns, goals, and values with family and medical staff

_____

_____

_____

_____

✦ Acknowledge client/patient feelings and help client/patient determine the meaning of the feelings

_____

_____

_____

_____

✦ Help the client/patient talk about topics that are particularly difficult

_____

_____

_____

_____

✦ Help identify any spiritual issues and, if appropriate, find a spiritual advisor (priest, chaplain, pastor, friend) to talk about issues

_____

_____

_____

_____

✦ Support the client/patient's discussions with family members and with medical staff

_____

_____

_____

_____

Exercise 2: End-of-Life Care and Multicultural Issues

Considering multicultural issues related to end-of-life concerns is important while working with clients/patients and their families. An expanded multicultural population in the United States increases the opportunity for case managers to work with individuals with different cultural origins. The beliefs and values that these individuals have are greatly influenced by their culture; this means that many clients/patients may have different meanings and traditions for the end of life and its care. The following case gives you an opportunity to think about cross-cultural issues that case managers may face when working with end-of-life care.

Part One

Wilma Martinez, a 67-year-old Spanish-speaking woman, has congestive heart failure due to inoperable coronary artery disease. She has been hospitalized three times during the past six months, even though she has reliably taken five medications daily. She seems distressed when her physician discusses advance directives and encourages her to designate a health care proxy. She says she wants "everything" done to help her survive. The patient's daughter usually accompanies her to clinic appointments and serves as translator. A few months after the discussion about advance directives, the physician asks more specifically about Mrs. Martinez's preferences of end-of-life care. This time, Mrs. Martinez's daughter expresses a strong desire that her mother not receive mechanical ventilation or cardiopulmonary resuscitation. It is unclear whether this represents a change in the patient's preferences or reflects the daughter's wishes [Crawley, Marshall, & Lo, 2002].

Source: Excerpt from "Strategies for Culturally Effective End-of-Life Care." Crawley, L. M., Marshal, P. A., Lo, B. and Koenig, B. A. May 7, 2002. *Annals of Internal Medicine,* 136(9): 673–679.

The physician comes to you as the case manager for Mrs. Martinez to ask the following questions. Respond as best as you can.

1. Explain in as much detail as possible what Mrs. Martinez's wishes are.

_____

_____

_____

_____

2. Is the daughter providing alternative directions for medical care? Can you give any reasons why the daughter responds the way she does?

_____

_____

_____

_____

Part Two

Wilma Martinez is a 67-year-old immigrant from El Salvador who moved to the United States to live with her daughter. Mrs. Martinez speaks only Spanish. Through her daughter's translations, the patient appears to comprehend details of her illness and treatment. When asked if she understands what the doctor is saying, she invariable nods affirmatively.

During a clinic visit when the patient's daughter is not present, the physician arranges for a trained medical interpreter to be present. When the physician discusses end-of-life preferences, the interpreter reports that Mrs. Martinez thought that ventilator support and cardiopulmonary resuscitation would hasten her death. Later, the interpreter explains that Ms. Martinez could not understand why staff were insistent that she, rather than her daughter, make decisions. Mrs. Martinez stated, "In my country, the family decides." Assuming that her daughter would make decisions for her, she saw no reason to sign forms. She worried that signing forms would cause legal problems because of her immigration status. The interpreter also suggests that Mrs. Martinez's nodding indicates politeness and respect for the physician, not assent.

The physician arranges for a trained interpreter to be present at subsequent clinic visits. By probing—for example, asking, "Tell me what you believe is going on in your illness"—the physician ascertains that Mrs. Martinez does not expect to survive her illness. By asking, "How would you like decisions to be made about your medical care?" the physician confirms that Mrs. Martinez wants her daughter to make decisions for her. Rather than assuming that Mrs. Martinez's nods signifying assent, the physician asks her specifically whether she has any questions or disagreements with the care plan [Crawley, Marshall, & Lo, 2002].

3. After reading Parts One and Two of this case, identify the issues: family disagreements, autonomy, and confidentiality. Discuss in detail the complications of the issues and how cultural considerations relate to each.

Family disagreements:

_____

_____

_____

_____

_____

Autonomy:

_____

_____

_____

_____

_____

Confidentiality:

_____

_____

_____

_____

_____

 # Exercise 3: Working with an Interpreter

 Return to the website that accompanies this book: www.thomsonedu.com/counseling/mcclam, Chapter 5, Link 1, "Working with Sign Language Interpreters in Human Service Settings," and review the role of the interpreter. Describe the role of the medical interpreter in Mrs. Martinez's case. Compare this interpreter's role with the role of sign language interpreters. What are the ethical issues involved in working as an interpreter and working with an interpreter?

_____

_____

_____

_____

_____

Exercise 4: Ethics and Managed Care

The advent of managed care emerged from the recognition that health care resources are limited and that allocation of these resources meant making some very difficult choices about care. A set of ethical principles can serve as guidelines for the interaction among managed care representatives, case managers (as well as other helpers), and clients/patients. This is true in health care and in mental health care. The following guidelines, if followed, promote better understanding and working relationships among the three parties (Povar et al., 2004):

- ✦ Relationships are critical in the delivery of services; they should include respect, truthfulness, consistency, fairness, and compassion.
- ✦ Health plans, those insured, clinicians, and the public share responsibility for "fair" use of resources.
- ✦ All parties involved in health care should foster an ethical environment of health care delivery.

What exactly do these guidelines mean in the day-to-day practice of the case manager? The following exercises will help you answer this question.

1. Write a short vignette about a teenager who has been receiving mental health treatment for approximately five years. End your vignette with a description of his current status and his parent's inability to receive additional funding for his treatment.

Five years of treatment:

_____

_____

_____

_____

_____

_____

_____

_____

_____

_____

Current status:

_____

_____

_____

_____

Denial of treatment:

_____

_____

_____

_____

2. Let's apply the guidelines presented above as a way of understanding how these guidelines are translated into a practical situation.

   The first guideline states "Relationships are critical in the delivery of services: should include respect, truthfulness, consistency, fairness, and compassion." In this case, this means that physicians, mental health providers, clients and parents, and managed care organizations need to be honest with one another. For example, (1) the managed care organization needs to be clear about the criteria required to cover certain treatments. (2) Professionals need to inform clients of their options regarding choices of care. (3) Clients and families need to present a fair representation of their specific mental health needs.

   Let's look at what this guideline means for your teenage client. The managed care policy for mental health needs state that the client/patient has a lifetime limit of $50,000 for services. The policy states these minimums:

   ◆ An annual minimum of 30 inpatient days ($17,160)
   ◆ An annual minimum of 20 outpatient visits ($1,440)
   ◆ A total annual limit of $18,600
   ◆ Total lifetime limit of $50,000 (Merrick et al., 2001)

   The services covered are inpatient psychiatric care, outpatient psychiatric care, intensive nonresidential care, and nonhospital nonresidential care.

3. Review and list the treatment that your teenage client has received for the past year and for the past five years and note what each of these treatments has cost based on the cost of services outlined above.

_____

_____

_____

_____

_____

4. Assuming that the managed care organization has already turned down the latest request for services, you, as the case manager, are advocating for your client. The managed care organization requires statements from each of the involved professionals and the client. Write a letter to the managed care organization. (Your client may not have used all of the resources available or may have far exceeded the minimums. Your request will differ from your classmates' requests because all vignettes are unique.)

Your letter of appeal:

_____

_____

_____

_____

_____

_____

_____

_____

_____

_____

_____

············· Exercise 5: A Global Perspective of AIDS

Global figures illustrate the serious nature of the HIV/AIDS epidemic. To prepare for the "In More Depth" section that follows, watch a link from "You Wake Me Up" at the website that accompanies this book, Chapter 10, Link 2.

1. What does the quote from Bono mean?

_____

_____

_____

2. Why is this epidemic particularly devastating to women?

_____

_____

_____

3. What does the content of this link mean to case managers in our country?

_____

_____

_____

In More Depth: The Ethics of AIDS

Today 17,000 people will die from AIDS-related causes. We continue to hear about the growing number of HIV-infected individuals worldwide, particularly in Africa. Approximately 4.9 million individuals worldwide will be infected this year, including 40,000 Americans. Growing trouble spots include Eastern Europe and Central Asia; in the United States, the problem is increasing among African Americans.

The subject of HIV (human immunodeficiency virus), the precursor of AIDS (acquired immune deficiency syndrome), is fraught with problems and conflicts about fears, treatments, rights, and responsibilities. Ethically, dilemmas arise in situations involving conflict between the rights or claims of a client and what the service provider, often a mental health and rehabilitation professional, feels about which rights or claims should prevail (Jordan & Meara, 1995). In some cases, competing client rights might result in a professional choosing a course of action that is supported by one or more ethical principles yet compromises others. These situations almost always involve complex legal issues and tough ethical dilemmas for service providers.

This "In More Depth" section will explore the ethical dimension of case management with clients living with HIV/AIDS to illustrate concepts introduced in Chapter 10 of *Generalist Case Management*. Although the chapter provides an overview of ethical dilemmas often encountered in case management, this discussion targets the dilemmas of service providers who work with this particular client group. As you read this section, we encourage you to remember that many situations do not have resolutions that are clearly right or wrong or that are specifically addressed by codes of ethics or ethical standards. Rather, a process of ethical decision making that includes consultation, supervision, legal considerations, and agency policy review is required and appropriate. The three areas of substantial ethical dilemmas identified by researchers are reviewed next (Garcia et al., 1999).

Professional Responsibility

Issues of professional responsibility include respect for client autonomy. An example is the client's right to make his or her own decisions except when such choices violate the rights of others. A client's decision to quit work and apply for disability benefits while able to work illustrates the dilemma the case manager faces about respecting client autonomy or confronting the client. Other client decisions that present dilemmas include refusing treatment, engaging in risky sexual practices, and abusing illegal substances. Client autonomy is also the premise for informed consent that requires case managers to inform clients about both treatment specifics and the limits of confidentiality. These important concepts require a balance between the disclosure policies of providers or agencies versus establishment of a helping relationship that feels safe to the client. An example of this dilemma is a mentally competent HIV-infected client who is rationally contemplating suicide.

Codes of ethics set forth the principle that case managers will do no harm to clients or to others, a concept derived from the Hippocratic oath. The question that arises with respect to clients living with HIV/AIDS is the following: What is the case manager's responsibility to a third party when the client refuses to disclose a positive HIV test to an unsuspecting sexual partner? The client has the right to protection of shared confidences; beaching confidentiality might result in harm to the client. At the same time, maintaining confidentiality may harm the third party. And therein lies the dilemma.

Competence

Codes of ethics address competence by stating that case managers should practice within their realm of education, training, and experience. When clients require expertise beyond that which case managers have, then case managers refer them to other professionals or agencies with the necessary expertise. Competence also requires recognition of the cultural and ethnic barriers of populations at risk and an understanding that the case manager may not be able to address these barriers. For example, professionals in the United States do not engage in service delivery when dual relationships may result. In other cultures, clients may only engage in helping when another relationship exists, perhaps as a close extended family member or friend.

Case managers are also limited in the scope of their practice with HIV-infected clients. For example, helpers do not deal with medical issues or concerns. Other conditions—for example, anxiety—may have a biomedical etiology rather than a psychological one. In such cases, the case manager would be limited in addressing the anxiety, particularly if the case manager is not part of a treatment team that includes a medical professional. Not referring the client to a medical provider may also result in problems for both the case manager and the client.

Confidentiality

A third issue identified by researchers is confidentiality and the duty to warn those who have or have had sexual contact with an individual with the virus. Should the case manager maintain confidentiality or take an active role in disclosure? In considering this question, the case manager must examine the implications for the helping relationship as well as the protection of others from harm.

There are four relevant issues related to confidentiality:

◆ Duty to maintain confidential information
◆ Potential problem of HIV-infected client injuring others
◆ Positions of professional associations on this issue
◆ Differing state laws

Although a number of professional organizations have not yet addressed this dilemma, the American Psychological Association has and makes the following recommendations (American Psychological Association, 1991). First, the psychologist (or the case manager in our example) must have knowledge of an identifiable at-risk, unsuspecting third party. Second, the case manager must have urged the client to notify the third party but the client has refused to do so. Finally, the case manager should be granted immunity from liability regarding good-faith decisions to disclose or refrain from disclosure to a third party. Some states, including Massachusetts and Florida, forbid disclosure of HIV status to third parties; other states allow some disclosure by certain professionals. And there are states where disclosure can result in criminal charges or civil suits.

Conclusion

Case managers who work with clients living with HIV/AIDS must be well versed in their organization's ethical standards and their agency's policies. They must also know the laws of the states in which they practice. And as suggested at the beginning of this section, practicing ethical decision making in situations lacking clear answers will facilitate the resolution of ethical dilemmas with the tough and complex issues that arise with this particular client group.

•••••••••••••• ● Exercise 6: HIV/AIDS Issues and Codes of Ethics

Read the sections of the Codes or Ethical Standards of American Counseling Association, National Association of Social Workers, or National Organization of Human Services that address professional responsibility, competence, and confidentiality. How does each of these relate to the ethical issues surrounding HIV/AIDS discussed in the previous section?

Professional responsibility:

_____
_____
_____
_____
_____

Competence:

_____
_____
_____
_____

Confidentiality:

_____
_____
_____
_____
_____

 # Self-Assessment

1. What strengths would you bring to an AIDS caseload?

_____
_____
_____
_____

2. What would be the most challenging aspects of a caseload of individuals with HIV/AIDS?

_____
_____
_____
_____
_____

3. What do you think about the global aspect of HIV/AIDS?

_____

_____

_____

_____

_____

4. When facing an ethical dilemma about HIV/AIDS or any other issue, what sources of help are available to you in addition to codes of ethics or ethical standards?

_____

_____

_____

_____

Pretest Answers

1. Patient's directive is followed if there is an advance directive; no directive? Then family decides; if irreconcilable differences, medical staff may ask court to intervene; medical staff makes decision if patient cannot speak and there is no one else to consult (p. 268).
2. Psychiatric settings, nursing homes, emergency departments, and outpatient settings (p. 270).
3. Dilemmas that arise about legislation, ethical codes, complex cases, technology, shared workspaces, using interpreters (pp. 271–274).
4. Occurs when helping professional must violate promised confidentiality to warn others that the client is a threat to self or others (p. 276).
5. Encouraging establishment of advance directives (medical power of attorney and a living will) and providing explanations of them (p. 285).

References

American Psychological Association (1991). Legal liability related to confidentiality and the prevention of HIV transmission. *Psychology and AIDS Exchange*, 7, 4.

Crawley, L. M., Marshall, P. A., & Lo, B. (2002). Strategies for culturally effective end-of-life care. *Annals of Internal Medicine, 136*(9), 673–679.

Garcia, J. G., Froehlich, R. J., Cartwright, B., Letiecq, D., Forrester, L. E., & Mueller, R. O. (1999). Ethical dilemmas related to counseling clients living with HIV/AIDS. *Rehabilitation Counseling Bulletin, 43*(1), 41–50.

Jordan, A. E., & Meara, N. M. (1995). Ethics and the professional practice of psychologists: The role of virtues and principles. In D. N. Bersoff (Ed.), *Ethical conflicts in psychology* (pp. 135–141). Washington, DC: American Psychological Association.

Lo, B., Quill, T., & Tulsky, J. Discussing palliative care with patients. *Center for Ethics and Professionalism*. Retrieved December 12, 2005, from http://www.acponline.org/ethics/lo.htm.

Merrick, E. L., Garnick, D. W., Horgan, C. M., Goldin, D., Hodgkin, D., Sciegaj, M. (2001). Employee assistance programs in Fortune 500 companies. *Psychiatric Services, 52*, 943–948.

Povar, G. J., Blumen, H., Daniel, J., Daub, S., Evans, L., Holm, R. P., et al. (2004). Ethics in practice: Managed care and the changing health care environment: Medicine as a profession managed care ethics working group statement. *Annals of Internal Medicine, 141*, 131–136.

Surviving as a Case Manager

The information in Chapter 11 of *Generalist Case Management* describes the real-life world of case managers throughout the nation, including the challenges they face and the survival skills they need. This chapter provides an opportunity to explore the world of the case manager and practice skills to face the difficulties.

 **Pretest**

1. Explain why a case manager needs to function as a "Jack or Jill" of all trades.

_____

_____

_____

_____

2. Provide three reasons why good organizational skills and communication skills help the case manager perform his or her job. Cite an example to illustrate each.

_____

_____

_____

_____

_____

_____

3. What do you think would be difficult about using ethical decision making during case management?

_____

_____

_____

_____

4. Describe three personal qualities that help case managers perform their tasks.

_____

_____

_____

5. Why are case managers vulnerable to burnout?

_____

_____

_____

6. What are three ways that you believe case managers can improve their time management skills?

_____

_____

_____

7. Why is assertiveness a difficult skill for a case manager to use?

_____

_____

_____

_____

Chapter Summary

The analysis of interviews with case managers from across the United States revealed eight common themes: the performance of multiple roles, organizational abilities, communication skills, setting-specific knowledge, ethical decision making, handling boundaries, critical thinking, and personal qualities. Because case managers are often required to function as advocates, coordinators, planners, and/or problem solvers, managing time and completing paperwork are critical skills to meet clients' needs. The case managers who were interviewed claimed that communication is more important than any other skill and is tied directly to establishing a helping relationship, assessing needs and situations, and selling and persuading clients. Because clients seek services whenever they are in need, the case manager has the responsibility of making sure that a client's best interests are always kept in mind.

The case manager can better meet the needs of the clients if he or she knows about services, systems, and terminology common in his or her particular setting. The case manager needs to maintain appropriate boundaries with the clients and make decisions that are ethically grounded. Being a case manager is demanding, and often case managers experience burnout because of the intensely emotional nature of their work. Effective case managers are patient, flexible, critical thinkers, and self-confident. Even so, helping others is difficult. As case managers continually face unsolvable problems, unmotivated clients, resistance, and bureaucracy, their ability to care is hindered. Acquiring time management and assertiveness skills can help case managers avoid burnout.

Exercise 1: "Jack or Jill" of All Trades

1. Review the job description of a case manager for a homeless shelter.

STATE-FUNDED JOB
DEPARTMENT OF PERSONNEL
CLASS SPECIFICATION

Class Title: **CHILD AND ADULT SERVICES CASE MANAGER 1**	Abbreviation: **CM 1**

SUMMARY: Under general supervision, is responsible for professional case management work of routine difficulty, and performs related work as required.

DISTINGUISHING FEATURES: This is the trainee/entry level class in the Child and Adult Services Case Manager job series. An employee in this class learns to perform a variety of case management duties.

EXAMPLE OF DUTIES AND RESPONSIBILITIES

Learns to provide case management services for homeless adults and families and communicates with service providers to obtain information regarding participation and improvement/status of adults and families receiving service; coordinates and documents progress in observable and measurable terms; makes recommendations for termination of aftercare when goals are met.

MINIMUM QUALIFICATIONS

Education and Experience: Graduation from an accredited college or university with a bachelor's degree.

Necessary Special Qualifications: (1) A valid motor vehicle operator's license is required. (2) Applicants for this class must have no conviction of a felony. (3) Applicants must be willing to be fingerprinted and must have their fingerprints on file. (4) Applicants must authorize release of any investigative and criminal records obtained by the Federal Bureau of Investigation. (5) Basic case management certification or successful completion of other required preservice training offered by the state within six months of an employee's appointment to this position.

EXAMINATION METHOD: Education and experience, 100 percent, for Career Service positions.

2. Based upon the job description you have just read and the information that you have gained from reading and studying Chapter 11 in *Generalist Case Management*, describe a day in your life at work assuming you have been hired for this case management position. You have been on the job for nine months, have a large client load, and provide direct services to homeless adults and families.

3. Re-read the day in the life of the case manager that you wrote in Item 2.

4. List three specific roles that you performed. Describe the specific tasks that are linked to each role.

_____

_____

_____

_____

_____

_____

_____

_____

5. Were you involved in problem solving? If so, describe the method of solving problems you used. If not, describe a situation in which you might use problem solving while working with homeless adults and children.

_____

_____

_____

_____

_____

_____

_____

6. Describe how any roles or tasks that you described in Item 4 create challenges for you as a case manager of homeless adults and children.

_____

_____

_____

_____

_____

_____

_____

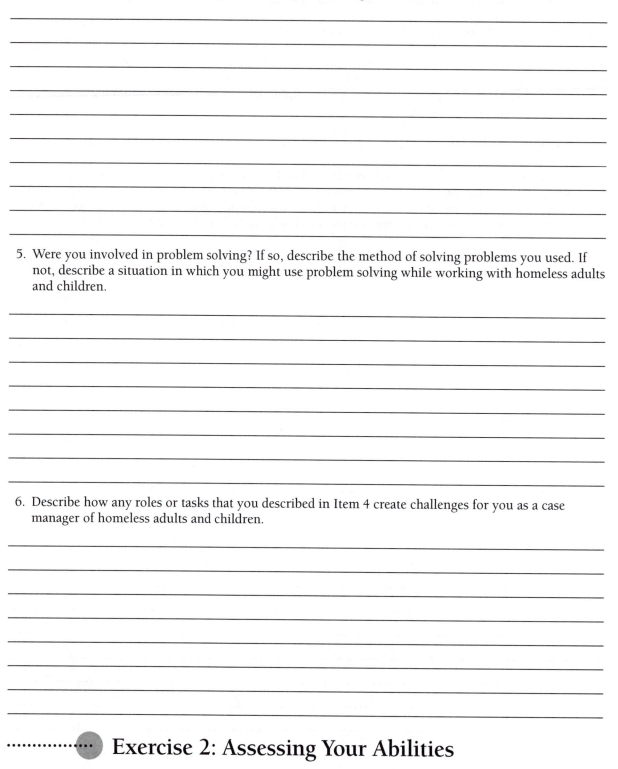

Exercise 2: Assessing Your Abilities

When you assume the role as case manager, you will be performing multiple roles or tasks. Using this self-assessment evaluation, think about how you might handle the responsibilities, rating yourself as poor (P), fair (F), or excellent (E). Describe previous situations where you have assumed these roles and what your experiences were.

Roles and Tasks	Self-Rating (circle one)	Description of Previous Experience
Advocate	P F E	
Broker	P F E	
Coordinator	P F E	
Planner	P F E	
Problem Solver	P F E	
Intensive Case Manager	P F E	
Crisis Case Management	P F E	
Moving Client to Self-Efficacy	P F E	

●············ ···● **Exercise 3: Assessing Your Personal Characteristics**

Case managers talk about personal characteristics they believe help them perform their jobs. This exercise will help you assess your strengths and explore the challenges you may encounter in relation to these characteristics.

1. In the following exercise, **circle** the characteristics you believe that you have and provide a specific example of a time when you demonstrated these characteristics.

2. Put a **box** around the characteristics you believe you have more difficulty demonstrating. Describe the barriers that exist for you with regard to the characteristics that present challenges.

Realistic:

_____

_____

Patient:

_____

_____

Flexible:

_____

_____

Self-confident:

_____

_____

Able to establish good relationships:

_____

_____

Assertive:

_____

_____

Sense of adventure:

_____

_____

Able to be a detective:

_____

_____

3. Read the case study in Chapter 11 of *Generalist Case Management* that describes Delores Fuentes's work with Mr. and Mrs. Ruiz to regain custody of their son Juan. Imagine that you, rather than Delores Fuentes, are the case manager in this case. Describe how the following personal characteristics will help you or challenge you as you work on this case.

Realistic:

_____

_____

Patient:

_____

_____

Flexible:

_____

_____

Self-confident:

_____

_____

Able to establish good relationships:

_____

_____

Assertive:

_____

_____

Sense of adventure:

_____

_____

Able to be a detective:

_____

_____

● Exercise 4: To-Do List

One of the most difficult challenges that case managers face is time management. Helpers often articulate the pressures they feel because they have large caseloads, work with clients with complex problems, assume administrative responsibilities, respond to crises, and work with limited resources. Many case managers maintain an ongoing to-do list that guides many of their activities for the day.

1. Review the "To-Do List: Monday" prepared by Sean, another case manager who works with homeless adults and families. Exercise 1 of this chapter describes his job.

TO-DO LIST: MONDAY

✦ Return three phone calls from yesterday from Sue at YWCA, Kim at Rehabilitation Unit, and Ms. Parks's psychologist.
✦ Lunch meeting with program committee of local social welfare organization.
✦ Check voice mail.
✦ Talk with supervisor about Sara Lee's need for surgery. Can the agency help with expenses?
✦ Prepare for staff meeting from 2:00 to 3:00 Tuesday.
✦ Dictate a case summary of Ida Johns.
✦ Write case notes on Joe Boyd and Kalisha Downs.
✦ Meet with Su Linn about her secretarial evaluation. Emphasize the importance of proofing her work and not gossiping with clients.
✦ Meet with Roscoe Kline and his wife for an intake interview.
✦ Arrange a psychological evaluation for Dean. Set up appointment and decide what information to send.
✦ Meet with Libby to tell her you can no longer help her with computer problems. Think about other alternatives.
✦ Begin work on proposal for work sample testing grant to assist clients with vocational placements.
✦ Update files on three clients seen yesterday: Rodriguez, Statlin, and Kosvoc.
✦ Read social history on Martha Wisten. Add to her file and review other reports received to date.
✦ Find clothes for Gloria's children.
✦ Schedule an intake interview for two clients, and their families, Brauns and Henrys.
✦ Make appointment for haircut.
✦ Review service delivery plan with co-worker Mr. Horowitz. Remember to get his signature.
✦ Attend meeting to discuss new drug and alcohol program and referral.

2. Assume that you are Sean. You have come to the office early Monday morning to make a plan for the day. Use the following planning form to outline the day's activities.

HOMELESS SERVICES CASE MANAGEMENT WORK LOG

Day: <u>Monday</u>

Time	Activity/Task	Notes	Follow-Up Activities
8:00–8:30			
8:30–9:00			
9:00–9:30			
9:30–10:00			

Continued

HOMELESS SERVICES CASE MANAGEMENT WORK LOG continued

Day: <u>Monday</u>

Time	Activity/Task	Notes	Follow-Up Activities
10:00–10:30			
10:30–11:00			
11:00–11:30			
11:30–12:00			
12:00–12:30			
12:30–1:00			
1:00–1:30			
1:30–2:00			
2:00–2:30			
2:30–3:00			
3:00–3:30			
3:30–4:00			
4:00–4:30			
4:30–5:00			

3. Now that you have made a plan for the day, review how you made your decisions about what "to do" by answering the questions that follow.

   (a) Were you able to fit all items on the To-Do List: Monday on the work log? Why or why not?

   _____

   _____

   _____

   _____

(b) What were your priorities? How did you establish these? Provide a rationale for determining your top two priorities. Explain why some tasks were less of a priority.

_____

_____

_____

_____

(c) How did you determine how long each task would take? What happens if each task takes 15 to 30 minutes longer than expected?

_____

_____

_____

_____

4. The plan that you constructed in Question 3 went well from 8:00 a.m. until 1:30 p.m. Unfortunately, you received a call at 1:30 p.m. from a client whose son was in a serious accident on the school playground. You met her at the hospital and stayed with her all afternoon and early evening. You called your sister and asked her to pick up your own two children from day care.

Tuesday morning you showed up at your office early to plan your day. After reading your e-mail, sorting through your in-box, listening to phone messages, and reading five messages from your supervisor, you begin a To-Do List: Tuesday

TO-DO LIST: TUESDAY

✦ Return e-mails from Monday.
✦ Fill out report for referral on Candace Sullivan's son
✦ Ask for help evaluating state information management system—due in two weeks.
✦ Return seven phone calls from yesterday.
✦ Plan Rob's (case manager's son) birthday.
✦ Find a time to meet with supervisor.
✦ Call hospital to find out medical status of client's son.
✦ Plan time for intake of two new cases.

You then combine Tuesday's list with the tasks on Monday's list that <u>did not get completed.</u>

✦
✦
✦
✦
✦
✦
✦
✦
✦
✦

7. What is your reaction to the growing list of tasks and the time available to work?

_____

_____

_____

_____

8. What do you think might happen in your agency when you cannot meet your clients' needs because of the time available?

_____

_____

_____

_____

9. How do activities such as establishing goals and priorities support time management?

_____

_____

_____

_____

● Exercise 5: Guidelines for Managing Time

Chapter 11 in *Generalist Case Management* provides guidelines for effective time management that present a way to approach the planning of each day. Review your plan for Monday and note if and how you used each guideline.

Guideline 1: The Responsibilities

◆ Pick the two most important goals and pursue them first

_____

_____

◆ Address the toughest jobs first

_____

_____

◆ Alternate difficult and easy tasks

_____

_____

◆ Group similar tasks

_____

_____

Guideline 2: The Planning of Time

◆ Plan some uninterrupted time

_____

_____

◆ Plan time for the unexpected or for crises

_____

_____

◆ Allot time according to deadlines

_____

_____

◆ Assign time to plan

_____

_____

◆ Assign time for paperwork

_____

_____

◆ Have a list of quick tasks to use as filler

_____

_____

Guideline 3: Time Management and Others

◆ Understand assignments

_____

_____

◆ Delegate tasks that others can or should do

_____

_____

◆ Develop a system for monitoring the work of others

_____

_____

◆ Say no when the assignment is inappropriate or there is not enough time to complete the task

_____

_____

⬤ Exercise 6: Time Management and You

After completing Exercises 4 and 5, answer the following questions focused on how you might address issues related to time management.

What do you think are the two most difficult time management issues you will face?

_____

_____

_____

_____

What guidelines will you use to manage your time? Explain why you chose these.

_____

_____

_____

_____

·············● Exercise 7: The Perspective of Case Managers

1. Go to the website that accompanies this book: www.thomsonedu.com/counseling/mcclam, Chapter 11, Link 1, to hear case managers talk about paperwork.

   ◆ What suggestions do they have for handling paperwork?

   _____

   _____

   _____

   _____

   ◆ What is the "bottom line" regarding paperwork?

   _____

   _____

   _____

   _____

2. Now go to Link 2. These four individuals share what they do to stay healthy.

   ◆ List some of their activities.

   _____

   _____

   _____

   _____

   ◆ List the activities you engage in to be healthy.

   _____

   _____

   _____

   _____

·············● In More Depth: The Cost of Caring

These days, traumatic events seem much more common: terrorist attacks, natural disasters like tsunamis, hurricanes, and fires, torture, acts of genocide, sexual victimization, school and workplace violence, and other events involving actual or threatened death or serious injury or a threat to self or others' physical well-being (American Psychiatric Association, 2000). Reactions to such situations usually include intense fear, helplessness, or horror and often lead to severe anxiety that was not present prior to the trauma. Today it is not only the client who is receiving attention; the reaction of helpers to client traumas is now also the focus of research. This in-depth section focuses on the relatively new field of psychotraumatology and the cost of caring experienced by helpers.

Historically, burnout, discussed in Chapter 11 of *Generalist Case Management*, has been used to characterize helpers' reactions to stress in the workplace. First described by Maslach in 1976, it is a process or condition of emotional exhaustion, depersonalization, and reduced personal accomplishments related to work that involves interactions with other people (Maslach, 1976). In the past, the term was all encompassing and included traumatic reactions as a form of burnout. More recently, terms such as compassion fatigue, empathic stress, secondary traumatic stress, and vicarious trauma have appeared as the preferred constructs to describe the emotional impact of working with trauma survivors specifically. *Vicarious trauma* has become the more popular term to describe the reactions of helpers that result from exposure to clients' traumatic experiences.

Vicarious Trauma

Although vicarious trauma and burnout share similar characteristics and may result in physical, emotional, and behavioral symptoms, work-related issues, and interpersonal problems, they are different in a number of ways (Trippany, Kress, & Wilcoxon, 2004). Vicarious trauma is the sudden traumatic reaction to specific client-presented information or experiences as opposed to the general psychological stress that typically describes the burnout experienced in helping professionals, which accumulates from working with challenging clients.

There are two sources of vicarious trauma. One is the emotional and psychological toll that results from the stress of responding to people in pain. This type of stress is unique to trauma work, cumulative in effect, and the most common incidence of vicarious trauma. The characteristics of an organization that contribute to stress are a second source of vicarious trauma. In the past, this type of stress has often been described as burnout; however, there is now recognition of stresses that are unique to trauma work and related to the organizational context in which the trauma work occurs. One of these contextual factors is the culture of the organization, particularly if there is no recognition of the effects of trauma on the helper. Distribution of workload among workers is a contextual factor that can minimize the risk of vicarious trauma by ensuring that no one helper only works with trauma survivors. Having a more diverse caseload is associated with decreased vicarious trauma (Chrestman, 1995). Other organizational factors that may contribute to vicarious trauma include the work environment, an absence of trauma-specific education, and lack of support from supervisors or co-workers.

How does a helper experience vicarious trauma? Repeated exposure to clients' traumatic experiences may cause a shift in the way helpers perceive themselves, others, and the world, profoundly affecting both the personal and professional life of the helper. Often helpers become witness to the very traumas that clients have experienced and may have a number of reactions, including feelings of being overwhelmed, fear, grief, horror, depression, anger, and pain. They may begin to experience nightmares and avoidance, changes in their own relationships, and tension and anxiety, all affecting their effectiveness with their clients. In addition, experiencing vicarious trauma has implications within the organizational context. Resignations due to vicarious trauma can result in high staff turnover and additional costs to find and train replacements; the loss of energy, commitment, and optimism among staff can have a depressing effect on the agency environment, and impaired helpers can compromise the quality and effectiveness of the organization's work.

Prevention of Vicarious Trauma

To be effective, prevention of vicarious trauma must occur at the same two levels of sources and effects. On an individual level, many of the techniques that are helpful with approaching burnout are also applicable to vicarious trauma among helpers. Exercise and other stress management techniques, supportive relationships with co-workers including peer support groups, continuing education, and counseling constitute strategies to maintain both physical and mental health. At the organizational level, creating a safe work environment recognizes the fact that helpers will be affected in some way by their work, particularly those working with trauma survivors. A helper's feelings may include ineffectiveness, powerlessness, and failure. Those managing organizations can create safe environments by encouraging vacations, starting peer support groups, varying caseloads, including health insurance that includes mental health coverage, and providing trauma-specific education. Effective supervision is also a critical component of the organizational response to vicarious trauma. In addition to emotional support, supervisors extend the safe environment by promoting relationships that allow helpers to express what they are feeling.

Both burnout and vicarious trauma are serious consequences of working in the helping professions. A helper who makes a conscious effort to be both physically and emotionally healthy will be more effective and productive and remain longer in the profession. The organization that recognizes the consequences of burnout and vicarious trauma will implement programs and strategies that address these concerns to remain effective and healthy organizationally.

Case Study: Alex's Story

Alex is a case manager at a local agency. She describes her work, the agency, and the challenges she faces as an Argentine in the United States:

I am from Argentina, and I have a BA in psychology from the University of Buenos Aires. I have experience working as a clinical psychologist in Buenos Aries. In 2000 I came to the United States where I studied English for two years at the university. I continue to take classes, and I am especially interested in minority groups, marginalization, poverty, cultural studies, racism issues, acculturation and assimilation between U.S. Hispanics, and language.

Today I am a case manager in a nonprofit organization that serves families in the region. My main job duties/responsibilities are assisting families with problems related to children's custody, including sexual abuse, domestic violence, and substance abuse problems, living skills, parenting skills, and anger management classes.

Working as a case manager gives me the opportunity to learn a lot about working with minorities. I received training for a month when I started at the agency; however, this agency constantly provides training in areas such as child development, psychological theories, sexual abuse, domestic violence, and substance abuse, independent living skills, parenting skills, and anger management.

The Agency

The agency has four residential and six outreach programs. Residential programs are for the following groups: pregnant teenagers; young women (13 to 18 years old) with serious behavioral and emotional problems who have suffered from abuse and neglect; adolescents who will live on their own or be reunited with their families; and teens at high risk for alcohol and drug treatment. The agency also has a number of outreach programs such as foster care, child and parenting skills, and education.

The program I work with is home based. Services are provided in the home to prevent disruption of the family unit so I assist families with children in crisis with the overall purpose of preserving the family unit. This program serves the county where I live and the 16 surrounding counties. The Department of Children's Services refers cases to us. We actually work for them. Once we receive a new case, we contact the DCS caseworker within 24 hours and the client within 48 hours.

We meet our clients at their home. Usually, the first contact we make with the client is by phone to schedule an appointment in the client's home; however, some of our clients have no phone so we go to their houses. Some of them are migrants, and unfortunately some of them are illegal foreigners. Most of them work in construction, fast food stores, or factories.

Most of the Hispanic clients live in trailers or projects in little towns. They cannot afford to rent an apartment or a house. The problem with clients living in trailers is that we have to enter a code to have access to the trailer area. Sometimes the code number does not work, and we have to wait until somebody who lives there opens the barrier. This makes our job very difficult. My best friend is "mapquest.com" a website that gives directions. However, some addresses cannot be found in this site.

Spanish is my first language so many people including those at my agency think that I can communicate with the clients who speak little or no English. Actually, most of them (not to say all of them) do not speak English; some speak very little English. Many of them do speak Spanish so I am able to communicate with them. But there are also many who speak a native dialect from Mexico or Guatemala or

Source: Case Study. Material from Maria Alejandra "Alex" Lopez. (2006). Unpublished manuscript. Knoxville, TN. Reprinted with permission.

other countries. As a result, they have limited ability to speak Spanish and some of them have spoken Spanish for only two or three years.

The First Meeting

The first interview includes several forms. Clients receive a statement about their rights and sign a release of information form. We need a client's permission to obtain information from other sources. Clients also receive a confidentiality statement. They are very concerned about confidentiality; however, building a relationship with them makes them feel more confident and safer. I also do a social assessment that includes very basic information, such as the full name, date of birth, Social Security number, age, school attending, and grade in school. More specific information that is quite comprehensive is also gathered. This includes the client's description of the problem, a social history of the client and the family, the family-of-origin history, educational history and current functioning, the current family relationship and proper history, peer/social relationships, employment history, mental health history, medical history, substance abuse history (client and family), legal history (being arrested/involved with court), and developmental delays or history if any.

We also begin an assessment plan that establishes two or three goals with the current date and a target date for completion. This is usually within three months. During this process, I am aware that some issues are very sensitive. Some clients are frightened to receive us in their houses. Although there are several reasons for this, a main reason is legal. Additionally, some clients do not know much about the Department of Children's Services, or my agency. They don't know much about the work I do for the agency, but once I tell them about what we do and what we don't do, they are open to disclosing their problems.

Most of my clients are defensive, skeptical, or even aggressive during the first interview. Some of them make up excuses, try to avoid me, do not answer the phone, and lie to me. However, they change their attitude in a relatively short time. In this point, I do not think that because I am Hispanic they can trust me immediately. It takes a while, sometimes two or three weeks (sometimes even more than that) to get their trust, but when they trust you, they trust you. They call me at my cell phone; they feel more comfortable discussing their issues; I am part of their lives.

If you were going to do my job, one of the most important things you need to know are cultural differences. I am from Argentina. My clients are from Mexico and other countries in Central America. Sometimes we are all called "Hispanic people" or "Hispanics" as a homogeneous group (perhaps because we speak Spanish?) disregarding the cultural differences in the Hispanic population that may include people from Mexico, Spain, or Latin America, who may come from big cities, or little towns, and who may speak Spanish or native dialects.

I come from Buenos Aires, which is a very "European" metropolitan city. We have strong influences from Spain, Italy, and France. So I don't have much in common with a client who comes from a rural area in Mexico and speaks a native dialect. Yet, many people call us Hispanics. Also, social class and lifestyle differences are two more important pieces. This means knowing the cultural values, preferences, dress, and priorities of your clients.

Challenges

There are several difficulties about my job. One of the most difficult things is the fact that case managers do not have a long time to work with each case. We keep a case open for approximately three months. So, many, many times, I find myself asking: What is/are the main goal/s in this case? Am I going to change this person/family's life in three months? Am I going to change the client's (bad) habits, addictions, financial issues, terrible cleaning habits, and terrible lifestyle in only three months? I wish I could, but I cannot.

One of the main duties/responsibilities of a case manager is connecting the client with community resources, depending on the client's needs. The client's community offers resources for several problems, such as housing, health, food, or financial issues. We develop a treatment plan along with the client, scheduling and performing individual and family sessions and providing direction and guidance to the client. We document the client's progress. This documentation may include client compliance, school performance, attendance, and verification of abstinence through urine screening. The client's behaviors and completion of the treatment plan will determine the length of treatment.

In some cases, the case manager's duty is much more than connecting clients with needed community resources. We can make a difference in the clients' life as case managers, but we must accept our limits as professionals. The clients have to be motivated to continue that change. I would like to share with you this short example to illustrate this:

> One of my clients was accused of drug issues and environmental neglect. A relative made an accusation against her. This person said that she was using and selling drugs, she was living in a dirty and unhealthy house, she had 12 cats, and the children were playing with the cats' feces, among other things. She was living with her two kids, her sister, and her sister's son. I went to the house. Her sister was extremely aggressive; she did not say hello, she did not want to talk to me, and she asked me to leave the house. Nobody wants a case manager coming to his or her house. The other sister tried to smooth things out and that is why I agreed to work with them. We do not visit people who do not want to work with us. If somebody asks us to leave the house, we close the case.
>
> The two sisters had to take two random drug tests to prove they were not using drugs. The tests were randomly assigned so it was hard to find them. We do not make appointments for random drug tests. We come by their houses, and they take the test. When the clients know they have a drug test appointment, they do not take drugs during that week or month. After a couple of weeks, they took the tests and passed them. So, I was supposed to close the case at that time; however, I did not feel comfortable closing the case. The house they were living in was a complete disaster. There were clothes, pieces of food, toys, and garbage everywhere. The children were extremely dirty. So, even if these clients were not using drugs, their children were not living in a neatly acceptable, clean environment.

The three months were over and I had to close the case, unless something about drugs was going on. Before I closed the case, I asked them to clean the house. I told them that the house was not clean, and they agreed with me to clean it. This is an example of the limitations we have. We call the DCS caseworker, meet at the client's house, verify that the drug tests are negative, and close the case, but we know that these clients did not change their poor lifestyle choice.

Another difficult situation is testing clients for the presence of drugs in their system and handling urine specimens or any hazardous material. Some agencies are not very careful about this. They do not follow the specific policies/regulations they have to follow, such as giving specific training to their employees, providing gloves to their employees, and taking all the precautions to protect their case managers.

Other difficult situations are the clients' limitations. Some people do the best they can; they do not have many resources to improve their lives. Some clients did not even finish elementary school so the chances of getting a better job are limited. They do not speak English, and some of them do not even speak Spanish. Basically, they are financially stressed and have few chances to change their financial situation.

Custody of children is a big piece in case management. A typical situation occurs when clients refuse to see me because the client knows/thinks/intuits that we are going to take their baby away. However, this is another misunderstanding. We do not take children away. The judge decides that.

Two other areas that are difficult for me are working with sex offenders and the language. Sometimes, I have a hard time trying to understand the various Spanish dialects that my clients speak and language is a real barrier.

Finally, there are a number of challenges about the job itself. First, I drive an average of 4,000 miles per month. Most of the clients are children who go to school or adults who work. So, most of my appointments are after 3:30 or 4:30 in the evening. Sometimes I get home around 10:00 or 11:00 p.m. This is very hard, and I get very tired. It makes for a long day. The other difficulty with my job is that I am on call 24/7. This means that if a client calls me during the weekend or at night, I have to assist him or her according to whatever the emergency is. Sometimes I can help clients over the phone, but there are times when I have to visit them.

Salary is another issue. Most agencies in this area pay between 11 and 15 dollars per hour. They do not pay overtime. We work more than 40 hours per week, but we do not get overtime. This is a high-risk job for several reasons: the places we travel, the amount of travel, the population with whom we work, and the responsibility we have. I work with an average of 15 cases each week. I spend (on average) two hours per week with each of my 12 to 15 clients; that is an average of 30 hours per week visiting clients. Basically, I think case managers are not paid according to the tremendous responsibility we have, the time this job takes, the effort we devote to our job.

Resistance

Resistance is a big piece in case management. Resistance appears in different ways. Some clients call me three or four times before the appointment, and then they do not show up. Some clients show up but do not comply with the treatment. They cannot make changes in their behaviors, relationships, education, financial situation, or lifestyle choices. Even though they are aware of their problems, they cannot change anything in their lives. There are several reasons for this resistance: lack of resources, lack of motivation, and lack of a social network to support those changes.

Many clients make up excuses, disconnect the phone, do not return my phone calls, or do not get the door when we have a scheduled appointment. We document each contact we make with the clients and each time we attempt to reach them. We leave a card with a note letting them know we were there. Sometimes they do not call me. I call them, and they say they did not call me because they cannot afford a long-distance phone call. I explain to them that there is a 1-800 number and they can call me at that number. My clients know that but refuse to call me.

We report these cases with a NS (no show) note. After a month of NSs, we close the case. I try my best to keep the cases open. I call them, talk with them, and explain to them that it is important for them to comply with the treatment. In many cases, they comply with the treatment; however, some clients remain resistant, and they do not want to comply.

A Difficult Case

A 12-year-old was raped by her cousin and became pregnant. The family was devastated. It was very hard to talk to them. Basically, they did not trust anybody. The parents do not speak English. The fact that I speak Spanish made them feel somewhat better but they were really uncomfortable. Every time we made an appointment, Mom asked me, "Are you going to ask me questions?" She was very defensive and skeptical. It was very hard to fill out the social assessment, the plan, and all the paperwork. I had to break it down and make it simpler. I also explained to them what the Department of Children's Services does and what the agency I work for does. They are illegal foreigners and were really afraid of any report we might make. Even though they never said that to me, I was able to perceive it. I explained to them that we do not report any illegal people. They thought about giving the baby up for adoption. After several conversations, they decided to keep the baby. I explained to them that they were the only ones (the 12-year-old and her family) to decide what to do with the baby. Nobody has the right to push them. After a couple of months working together, the baby was born and they decided to keep her. She was premature; the 12-year-old had an infection, and the baby was delivered after 7 months. The baby will be in an incubator for a month or more. The 12-year-old has pneumonia. We are still working together to make sure that the mother has all she needs and the baby is okay.

.... ● Exercise 8: Alex and Case Management

How are the eight common themes that characterize case management today illustrated by Alex?

Performance of multiple roles: _____

_____

_____

_____

Organizational abilities: _____

_____

_____

_____

Communication skills: _____
_____
_____
_____

Setting-specific knowledge: _____
_____
_____
_____

Ethical decision making: _____
_____
_____
_____

Handling boundaries: _____
_____
_____
_____

Critical thinking: _____
_____
_____
_____

Personal qualities: _____
_____
_____
_____

·············● Exercise 9: The Cost of Caring

1. What do you think would lead to burnout in Alex's job?

_____
_____
_____
_____

2. Imagine that Alex is suffering from vicarious trauma. What might cause this in her job?

_____

_____

_____

_____

3. What would be challenging for you in this job?

_____

_____

_____

_____

4. Alex is from Argentina so she is similar to her clients in some ways. How would this job be different for a case manager who is not from Central or South America—for example, a Caucasian, an Asian American, or an African American?

_____

_____

_____

_____

5. Can you think of any ways to do this job more effectively?

_____

_____

_____

_____

6. Would you want a job like this? Why or why not?

_____

_____

_____

_____

•••••••••••••• Exercise 9: Year 2005

1. Go to the website that accompanies this book, Chapter 11, Link 3, to read "Year of Suffering: Disasters Dominate 2005" by Erin McClam.

2. What are the traumas that occurred during 2005?

_____

_____

_____

_____

_____

3. Describe your own reactions to the suffering that has occurred.

_____

_____

_____

_____

4. Which of the crises would have been most challenging for you as a case manager? Explain the reasons for your choice.

_____

_____

_____

_____

_____

•••••••••••••• Self-Assessment

1. What strengths do you bring to the job of case manager?

_____

_____

_____

_____

_____

2. What would be the most challenging aspects of case management for you?

_____

_____

_____

_____

_____

3. Review Alex's Case Study in the "In More Depth" section. In what ways can you identify with Alex and the description of the work she does? In what ways are you unfamiliar with the issues she discusses and the reactions that she has?

_____

_____

_____

_____

 Pretest Answers

1. Performance of multiple roles (p. 295).
2. a) clients suffer because needs aren't met; b) completing paperwork provides records, an audit trail, and requests for services; c) communication is necessary to establish a helping relationship (pp. 295–297).
3. Confidentiality issues, immigration issues, and role conflicts (p. 298).
4. Realistic, patience, flexibility, self-confidence (pp. 299–300).
5. Unsolvable problems, unmotivated clients, the bureaucracy, psychological injury, lack of needed skills (p. 305).
6. Determine goals, prioritize, and plan (p. 309).
7. Difficult to say no to clients and colleagues because of their commitment to help others (p. 311).

 References

American Psychiatric Association. (2000). *Diagnostic and statistical manual of mental disorders* (4th ed., rev.). Washington, DC: Author.

Chrestman, K. R. (1995). Secondary exposure to trauma and self-reported distress among therapists. In B. H. Stamm (Ed.), *Secondary traumatic stress: Self-care issues for clinicians, researchers, and educators* (pp. 29–36). Lutherville, MD: Sidran.

Maslach, C. (1976). Burn-out. *Human Behavior, 5*(9), 16–22.

Trippany, R. L., Kress, V. E. W., & Wilcoxon, S. A. (2004). Previous vicarious trauma: What counselors should know when working with trauma survivors. *Journal of Counseling and Development, 82,* 31–37.